Volume Two:
Fascinating Tales
From
Obscure History

James R. Olson

Erian Press
Pittsburg, Texas

DEDICATION

To everyone who believes history should not only
educate, but also entertain and amuse.

CONTENTS

INTRODUCTION

This second volume of fascinating tales continues where volume one left off. If you read volume one, you realize these stories are collected from weekly emails I send to a list of readers enrolled from my web site, booksbyolson.com. To appreciate the stories you probably should understand my definition of obscure history.

Obscure history is the little known or seldom remembered tales about heroes or villains, real people just like you and me, who have made a mark in history, which, for whatever reason has been allowed to slip into obscurity. If you should happen to encounter these people in the history books, they are usually represented as a footnote, rating only a sentence or two. Yet these people, or animals, have done something that caused their names to be etched in the annuals of time.

In this volume you will encounter men and women, dogs and cats, commoner and royalty who have left their mark in obscure history. Our goal is to bring them a bit of the recognition they have earned. You may have heard of some of these events or characters, but chances are you'll meet them for the first time in these pages.

In *A Canadian Hero* you'll meet Gander, a Newfoundland dog who gave his life so his fellow soldiers would live.

President Theodore Roosevelt declared *Sergeant Henry Johnson* one of the bravest Americans to take up arms in World War I. Learn why he didn't receive the recognition he deserved until

2015.

You may have heard of King Arthur and *The Sword in the Stone*, but did you know there actually is a sword embedded in stone which you can see today at Monte Siepi Chapel in the San Galgano Abbey in Tuscany?

Learn the story of *The Flying Feminist*, the first woman to build and fly her own airplane, but has disappeared into obscure history.

Most likely you've read or heard about dogs who've traveled great distances to be reunited with their owners. I'll bet you've never heard about *The Amazing Journey of Clementine Jones*, the cat who traveled over 1600 miles to find her owners.

Did you hear the story of *The Youngest Hero* who became a decorated Navy World War II veteran when he was only twelve years old?

These are only a small sampling of the stories in this volume. Come with us to meet the spies, warriors, dogs, cats, artists, and inventors who have risen from the depths of obscure history to amuse and amaze us.

James R. Olson

A CANADIAN HERO

If you've ever seen a Newfoundland dog, you know a Newfie is a large working dog, with the males standing 28-29 inches and weighing around 130 – 150 pounds. This sweet tempered breed typically gets along very well with children but a Newfie may not always realize its size and strength. You have to appreciate that in order to understand how "Pal" became a war dog.

As part of the Hayden family, the gentle Newfie adored playing with the neighbor kids who often had him pull their sleds. During one playtime, however, "Pal" accidentally scratched a six year old with his big paw, and because the deep scratch required a doctor, the Haydens were faced with putting Pal down, or giving him away. They chose life for the 130 pound dog, and that's how Pal became the regimental mascot for the 1st Battalion of the Royal Rifles of Canada.

The Royal Rifles stationed at Gander International Airport quickly welcomed the dog into their ranks. The soldiers renamed him Gander and "promoted" him to sergeant. When the unit was shipped to Hong Kong in the fall of 1941, Sergeant Gander went along.

Hong Kong was very hot and Gander's thick, heavy coat wasn't well suited to the climate. To help Gander cope with the heat, Rifleman Fred Kelly (Gander's handler) let him take long cold showers. The Newfie was also reported to have a fondness for cool beer.

Gander, however, developed a dislike of Asians, probably related to the efforts of some locals to steal him. He got away, but only after a struggle, and Gander never forgot. His regiment didn't discourage Gander's snarling and snapping, and this may explain why Gander had such a ferocious reaction to the invading Japanese.

On December 7th, the Japanese attacked Pearl Harbor, and eight hours later, Japanese troops poured across the border to engage British, Indian, and Canadian units on Hong Kong Island. Armed only with his formidable size and an intimidating set of teeth, Gander fought alongside his fellow Canadians. The large dog charged and tackled any Japanese soldier who got too close to his Canadian troops. "He growled and ran at the enemy soldiers, biting at their heels," recalled Rifleman Reginald Law. Since most of the fighting occurred at night, Gander's black coat made him all but invisible, and instead of shooting the enormous dog, the Japanese beat a hasty retreat to avoid the "black beast." Gander's fierce attacks drove back the Japanese troops at least twice.

During the battles both sides threw grenades which injured or killed many soldiers. On the fifth or sixth day of battle Gander was guarding a group of wounded Canadians when a Japanese grenade landed in their midst. The big dog instantly picked up the grenade in his massive jaws and ran it back toward the Japanese. No one will ever know for certain whether Gander realized the grenade was deadly, but if he didn't think it was dangerous, why would he run it back to the Japanese? Although Gander was killed in the explosion, he had saved the lives of at least seven soldiers.

The allied forces had no reasonable chance of winning the battle, but the Canadians fought valiantly, finally surrendering on December 25th (Black Christmas). When the Japanese interrogated Canadian prisoners they were particularly interested in learning about the "Black Beast", because they were concerned the Allies were training vicious animals for combat.

By the time the war ended Gander had been forgotten by everyone except the Canadian POWs. It took nearly 60 years and efforts by various veterans groups before Gander received his first official recognition. On October 27, 2000 the PDSA (the UK's leading veterinary charity) posthumously awarded Gander the Dickin Medal, the first such award since 1949, and to the best of my knowledge, the only award for an animal killed in the line of duty. The Dickin Medal is often referred to as the animal equivalent of the Victoria Cross (Britain's highest award for valor). The medal was accepted by Fred Kelly, Gander's former handler, in the presence of thirty-five Hong Kong veteran POWs who attended the ceremony. The citation read:

> "For saving the lives of Canadian infantrymen during the Battle of Lye Mun on Hong Kong Island in December 1941. On three documented occasions, Gander, the Newfoundland mascot of The Royal Rifles of Canada, engaged the enemy as his regiment joined The Winnipeg Grenadiers, members of Battalion Headquarters "C" Force and other Commonwealth troops in their courageous defense of the island. Twice Gander's attacks halted the enemy's advance and protected groups of wounded soldiers. In a final act of bravery, the war dog was killed in action gathering a grenade. Without Gander's intervention, many more lives would have been lost in the assault."

Gander has achieved a degree of immortality in Canada. Surviving prisoners insisted Gander's name be listed with the 1,975 men and two women when the Hong Kong Veterans Memorial Wall was unveiled on August 15, 2009 in Ottawa, Ontario, Canada. The Forgotten Heroes monument, dedicated on July 2, 2012 at the Cobequid Veterans Memorial Park in Bass River, Nova Scotia, includes a statue of Gander by Nova Scotia sculptor Clifton Sears. Statues of Gander and his handler were unveiled on July 23, 2015 at Gander Heritage Memorial Park in Gander, Newfoundland.

As of 2015, Gander remains Canada's only decorated military animal. It will be a long time before he is forgotten.

A MIDNIGHT RIDE

One of the marvels of the human condition is the ability of ordinary people to do extra ordinary things. This is the story of a sixteen year old girl who carved her place in history by performing one of those extra ordinary deeds.

Sibyl Ludington was born April 5, 1761 in the small town of Fredericksburg, New York near the border between the colonies of New York and Connecticut. She was a bit of a tom boy, and by the time Sibyl was a teenager she could ride as well, if not better, than any boy in the neighborhood.

The 1770s were an exciting and scary time to be alive. The American colonies were in open revolt against the tyranny of King George III. The Battles of Lexington and Concord, the first military engagements of the American Revolutionary War, had been fought on April 19, 1775. On June 17, 1775 the colonial forces had fought the British at the Battle of Bunker Hill near Boston. On July 4, 1775 a group of colonists had met in Philadelphia and penned a letter to the King, proclaiming independence for the colonies.

In early April, 1777 war had not yet reached Fredericksburg, but because her father, Henry Ludington, was a New York militia officer Sibyl frequently listened to the officers discuss the conflict over the dinner table. It was only a matter of time until the British troops intruded upon their peaceful existence. Consequently plans were developed for how the militia would respond to such an invasion.

The militia under Henry Ludington's command was comprised mostly of farmers without any formal military training. Although the militiamen's farms were spread over a wide area, they were fervent patriots, ready on short notice to take up arms in defense of the idea of freedom from a tyrannical foe.

On the stormy Saturday evening of April 26th, the message Colonel Ludington had anticipated, and feared, arrived via courier. The British had sacked and burned the town of Danbury and were advancing toward Fredericksburg. The members of Ludington's militia were scattered around the countryside preparing for Sunday's day of rest and worship. The Colonel had a quandary. Plans had anticipated more time to contact and assemble the militia, but Ludington needed a courier immediately. The military courier who had brought the message was already exhausted and unable to carry the message to the scattered militia. He couldn't alert the militia himself because he needed to stay at his residence to muster the troops as they arrived.

The chaos of the messenger's arrival had awakened Sibyl. When she realized the situation, Sibyl immediately volunteered to ride to arouse the sleeping militia. Ludington had doubts about the wisdom of sending a sixteen year old girl off on such an important and dangerous mission, but he obviously had no reasonable choice if the militia were to protect their homes and farms.

Just a few minutes before midnight, Sibyl put a man's saddle on her pony, Star, and began her historic ride. She galloped through the stormy night along muddy roads, shouting the message that the British had sacked and burned Danbury and the militia should gather at Colonel Ludington's home before dawn.

By daybreak, an exhausted Sibyl arrived home, drenched to the skin and covered with mud, but she had successfully completed her mission. Nearly the entire regiment was mustered at her father's house where they organized and prepared to march out to join General Gold Selleck Silliman's small army. At the Battle of Ridgefield on April 27, 1777 the patriots were able to stop the British advance and push them back to their boats. (In

December, 2019, the grave of three men, believed to have been casualties from the Battle of Ridgefield were discovered under the foundation of an 18th Century home.)

Nearly every school child is familiar with the midnight ride of Paul Revere who roused the colonists against the British troops marching toward Lexington and Concord. There are probably several reasons why no one remembers, or has even heard about, Sibyl Ludington's epic ride. Paul Revere was a well known personality in the political hotbed of a large city—Boston, while Sibyl was an unknown girl from a small backwoods community. The battle following Revere's ride was the shot heard around the world, and set off the war of rebellion. The battle following Sibyl's ride was merely another skirmish is a long and bloody conflict.

Although mostly forgotten, Sibyl's ride was by far the longer —forty miles—three times as long as Revere's ride. Young Sibyl could boast she had avoided capture by the British, while Paul Revere had indeed been captured.

On October 21, 1784 Sybil married Edmund Ogden, a sergeant in a Connecticut regiment, and afterward lived in Unadilla, New York. They had one son, Henry Ogden, who became a lawyer and a New York State Assemblyman. Edmund died on September 16, 1799. Sibyl continued living in Unadilla until her death on February 26, 1839.

Sibyl's story was resurrected in the 1980s, when the growing feminist movement chose her life to highlight the way women's roles in history have been forgotten or downplayed. When the feminists compared Sibyl's ride favorably to Paul Revere (three times as long as Revere's ride, and she wasn't captured by the British), the story was attacked as fraudulent and feminist-biased. In 1996, the Daughters of the American Revolution (DAR) even refused to put a marker on Sibyl's grave, which would have recognized her as a patriot hero.

When historical records confirmed Sibyl's amazing ride had actually occurred, the DAR changed its mind. In 2003 a marker was placed on Sibyl's grave finally granting her at least a small measure of the recognition she deserved.

A RELAY RACE
AGAINST DEATH

It was January 1925 when Dr. Curtis Welch diagnosed six-year-old Richard Stanley's illness—it was diphtheria, a disease that attacks the throat and blocks the respiratory passages and is nearly always fatal. Within 24 hours Richard Stanley was dead and several new cases had been reported. Dr. Welch knew if he didn't receive a supply of anti-diphtheria serum an epidemic would sweep through the little town of Nome, Alaska.

Getting supplies of the serum to Alaska from the United States was a relatively simple matter. Getting those supplies to Nome in January was another story. The nearest railroad station to Nome was at Nenana, more than 1,000 miles away. Between the two towns lay a wilderness of snow, ice, and forest, through which the fastest transport was sled and dog team. Under ideal conditions the trip took at least two weeks. Nome could not afford a two week delay in receiving the desperately needed serum.

On January 27, two days after the outbreak was first reported a plea for help from Nome's mayor, George Maynard, was headlined in newspapers throughout the northeast. On the same day a tall, bearded trapper, Wild Bill Shannon suggested the trip to Nome could be made in one week instead of two by doing it in relays. Between Nenana and Nome were fifteen small trading posts. At each post was an experienced trapper who could be called on to help.

Shannon volunteered to take the serum to the first post where he would hand it over to begin the relay of trappers who would drive themselves and their dogs to the limits, day and night. That afternoon, when a metal case containing 30,000 units of serum arrived in Nenana, Shannon secured it on his sled and set out for the first post on the relay, Tolovana, 50 miles away.

He drove his huskies mercilessly, hour after hour. Darkness brought bitter cold and a razor-edged wind. You have to experience 30 and 40 degree below zero temperatures to appreciate how deadly they can be. Even with heavy clothing the cold seeps into your bones, making every movement an act of will power. Every breath you take feels as if your lungs are on fire. Your body cries for you to curl up and go to sleep—a sleep you know you'll never awaken from.

Just before midnight Shannon reached Tolovana where his exhausted dogs collapsed in the snow. With his face and eyes rimmed with ice, half blind, Shannon handed the serum off to trapper Dan Green who immediately set out with his own team toward Manley Hot Springs, another 50 miles along the trail.

Meanwhile, another team, driven by Leonhard Seppala, who was reputedly the fastest teamster in that part of the territory, had set out from Nome toward Nenana. Unaware help was on the way, Seppala had decided to make a dash for Nenana, pick up the serum, and try to make the 1,000 mile return trip nonstop, relying on fresh dog teams picked up at the trading posts.

By daybreak on January 31, Seppala had covered 200 miles when through eyes bleary with fatigue, he saw another team approaching. It belonged to Henry Ivanoff, who had set out from the post at Shaktolik the previous day and was suffering badly from frostbitten feet. Seppala took the serum and headed back toward Nome.

It was an agonizing journey for his stalwart dogs. When the team was halfway across the frozen waters of Norton Sound, a blizzard swept down. The swirling whiteness blotted out everything, forcing Seppala to rely on instinct alone as he pushed his dog team onward.

Early on February 1 Seppala reached the far side of the sound and the tiny settlement of Golovino, 100 miles from Nome. The snow, ice, and subzero temperatures had taken their toll of both man and dogs. Reluctantly, Seppala handed over the serum to prospector Charlie Olson.

At the small village of Bluff, Olson passed over the serum to another prospector, Gunnar Kaasen, who would carry the life saving serum the final seventy miles to Nome. At 5:30 on the morning of February 2, with a snowstorm raging, Kaasen reached the outskirts of Nome. The dogs collapsed and Kaasen —his face torn by iced particles, temporarily blinded, and almost unconscious— had to be chipped from the sleigh. The serum, now a frozen block, was delivered to Dr. Welch in time to avert disaster. Apart from little Richard Stanly, the terrible epidemic of diphtheria had claimed only one other victim.

The epic race—1,000 miles of mountain, forest, and valley, through storm and gale-force winds, in temperatures of 50° below zero—had taken five-and-a-half days, cutting the previous speed record nearly in half. Four dogs died from exposure, giving their lives so others could live.

Since 1973, to honor the memory of the courageous men and dogs who had made the serum run, the Iditarod Trail Sled Dog Race, of 938 miles from Anchorage to Nome, is held each March and is run on some of the same trails beaten by more than 150 dogs and 20 drivers who participated in the relay race against death.

BATTLE OF HAYES POND

You may never have heard of the Lumbee Indian nation, which is located mostly in North Carolina. They are the largest tribe east of the Mississippi River and the ninth largest Indian tribe in the U.S. Their population is centered in Robeson County, North Carolina, which is where our little story begins.

Most people think of segregation as separating white and black, but Robeson County's population had been split in three (white, black, and Indian) since the 1880s. The county had three sets of buses, three separate water fountains and three school systems—all closely watched by the Ku Klux Klan.

Things were starting to change in Robeson County, and the Klan wasn't happy about it. Brown v. Board of Education had recently outlawed school segregation throughout the United States. Locally, the Lumbee Tribe had been formally recognized by the state of North Carolina. Being the bullies they are, the Klan felt obligated to show everyone who was really in charge. On the night of January 13, 1958, two crosses burned in Robeson County. One was outside the home of a Native American woman who was dating a white man, and the other was in front of the home of a Native family who had moved into one of Lumberton's all-white neighborhoods.

The latest cross burnings were KKK Grand Dragon James W. "Catfish" Cole's wake-up call to alert the citizens to the Klan's shining moment, its chance to "put the Indians in their place, to end race mixing." The KKK put up fliers advertising a rally and cross burning to be held that weekend in a cornfield Cole had rented from a local farmer.

On Saturday morning Robeson County Sheriff Malcolm McLeod looked up Catfish Cole and asked him to cancel the rally, but the Grand Dragon refused. The atmosphere was very tense all day throughout the county. It seems everyone realized something unpleasant was going to happen.

The first Klansmen arrived on the frigid field at 7 p.m., an hour and a half before the rally was scheduled to start. All were armed, and most donned winter jackets since the temperature was supposed to drop into the 20s that night. The Klansmen also brought a cross, a large banner emblazoned with three red K's, and a single light bulb on a pole. A public address system was setup on a flatbed truck used as a makeshift stage. Cole waited eagerly for an anticipated crowd of about 500 Klan members to arrive. Only about 50 actually turned out. Perhaps they realized the Indians weren't going to be intimidated.

Meanwhile, a group of Lumbees waited in their cars nearby. The Klansmen's broadcasts and flyers had done their job. In addition to the local residents, there were also Lumbees who had made the journey home just to confront the KKK. By 8:15 p.m., 300 to 400 Lumbee tribe members had arrived and vastly outnumbered the Klansmen. The Klan was almost always a majority for their intimidating cross burnings.

Sheriff McLeod cautioned Catfish Cole to keep the confrontation under control. "I can't control the crowd with the few men I've got," McLeod said.

Disregarding the sheriff's warning, Cole and the Klansmen continued to taunt the Indians with racial slurs. Just before the rally was scheduled to begin Lumbee member Neill Lowery shot out the single light bulb, extinguishing the field's only light source. As the field plunged into darkness, the scene turned to chaos. Suddenly the area was lit by flashes of gunfire. Witnesses were certain several thousand rounds of ammunition were fired.

Catfish Cole ran for his life into the nearby swamps, followed by other Klansmen who hurriedly drove or ran away from the field. In Cole's haste to get away, he left his wife behind, in their car. His panicked wife got stuck in a ditch while attempting to leave the field, but Lumbee Indians graciously helped to free her car. Sheriff McLeod, along with State Highway Patrol Captain Raymond Williams and their officers, stepped onto the field, firing tear gas into the crowd.

It only took a few minutes for the tear gas to dissipate from the suddenly empty and quiet field. The Klansmen were either driving away or dashing through the swamps. Although hundreds of shots had been fired, there were no known casualties. The Lumbees had intentionally fired into the air attempting to scare the KKK. It was suspected the KKK never returned fire because they were too busy trying to get away,

The battle's story was picked up by news outlets nationwide in publications like *Life* magazine, the *Los Angeles Times* and the *New York Times*. The media praised the Lumbees' victory and didn't have any good things to say about the KKK.

Grand Dragon James "Catfish" Cole was arrested and a mixed race jury found him guilty of inciting a riot. He was sentenced to 18 to 20 months in prison. The Klansmen never returned to Robeson County.

In July 2018, a historical marker was erected at N.C. Highway 130 and Hayes Pond Road, reading:

> "Battle of Hayes Pond: The Lumbee and other American Indians ousted the Ku Klux Klan from Maxton, Jan. 18, 1958, at rally 1/2 mile west."

Now you know the entire story.

CHARLIE MCCOMAS

People's fascination with mysteries probably accounts for the continuing interest in the legend of the red-haired, white Apache war chief. This is the story of that legend.

The McComas family was one of the most prominent in the territory. In 1880, when his political career was at its height, H.C. McComas relocated his family to Silver City, New Mexico after receiving an appointment as federal judge.

March 27, 1883, was such a fine spring day Judge McComas decided to make a family excursion of his judicial journey to Leitendorf, New Mexico, a small mining camp near Lordsburg. Since the buckboard was too small for the entire family, he included only his wife and their six year old son, Charlie, leaving their two daughters, aged eight and twelve, in Silver City.

The first day of the journey passed pleasantly as the buckboard moved leisurely through the flowering hills. At Mountain Home, a wayside haven about halfway between Silver City and Lordsburg, the McComas family stopped for the night. Although communications on the frontier was generally poor, information about hostile Indians spread readily. The talk at Mountain Home was all about the raiding band of hostile Apaches, who had crossed into southeastern Arizona on March 21st, killing at least sixteen men in a series of raids. Judge McComas wasn't particularly worried since all the Apache attacks were well west of Silver City and Lordsburg.

The next morning the three buckboard passengers were enjoying a pleasant spring outing until they reached a point about ten miles from Mountain Home, where they blundered into a raiding party of hostile Chiricahua. When Judge McComas saw the dozen mounted warriors, he reacted immediately. He jerked on the reins, turning the buckboard back toward Mountain Home. Handing the reins to his startled wife, he grabbed his rifle and leaped to the ground, prepared to give his life to buy time for his wife and son to escape. Within seconds Judge McComas fell, riddled with bullets.

The retreating buckboard had traveled only about 500 feet when one of the horses screamed and collapsed, mortally wounded. The frantic Mrs. McComas swept her son into her arms, jumped to the ground, and attempted to escape on foot. About thirty yards from the buckboard the raiders swooped down on her. Charlie was snatched from his mother's protective arms as the butt of a rifle crushed Mrs. McComas' skull.

Although the terrain around the massacre scene was thoroughly searched for a radius of a mile, no evidence of Charlie McComas could be discovered. For several days various volunteers combed the hills with equally discouraging results. The searchers finally concluded young Charlie had been carried off by the raiders. Apaches frequently kidnapped children, intending to raise them as members of their tribe.

The McComas tragedy was the spark necessary to fire the citizens of the Southwest and create a national sensation. Newspapers around the country raised a cry for the Army to cross the border, clean out the nest of hostiles, and recover Charlie McComas.

On May 1st American troops crossed the Mexican border in pursuit of the hostile Apaches. On the afternoon of May 15th the soldiers struck an Apache rancheria, killing and capturing several of the hostiles. Interrogation of the captives disclosed Charlie McComas had been in the village at the time of the attack, but had run away with an old squaw. Other squaws, who returned to the captured rancheria to surrender, confirmed the story, with the additional information that Charlie had escaped, running terror-stricken into the depths of the mountains. An immediate search for the boy was begun. The country was so rough and the timber and brush so thick his tracks could not be followed. A violent rain storm during the succeeding night ended all hope of finding Charlie.

The story of the McComas tragedy should rightfully have ended at this point. But since Charlie's body was never recovered, there were rumors the boy might have survived with one of the families of Apaches who had remained deep in the mountains.

As the major participants in the McComas tragedy died, Charlie was forgotten by all but a few old timers. Than on April 10, 1930, a band of hostile Apaches attacked a ranchero near Nacori Chico, Sonora, Mexico, and killed three persons. These wild Apaches were evidently part of a small band which had remained hidden in the vastness of Mexico's Sierra Madre Mountains, never surrendering their precious freedom. Soon rumors began to circulate that the renegade band had been led by a red-haired white man about 50 years old. If Charlie McComas had been alive in 1930, he would have been 53 years old.

For many years rumors about an aged white man leading the Chiricahua spread throughout the southwest. A major magazine even published a story about the existence of these wild Apaches and their white Apache leader. For the romantically inclined, this white man could be none other than the long lost Charlie McComas.

Finally, in 1959, Jason Betzinez, who had been a novice warrior with the renegades during the Apache campaign of 1883, told his story. Since the persons directly involved were now dead, he felt no harm would be done in telling the true story of Charlie McComas' fate. According to Betzinez, during the May 15th attack on the Apache camp an Apache warrior named Speedy had been so enraged by his mother's death; he turned and brutally killed Charlie, stoning the boy to death. The Chiricahua had told the story about Charlie running off in order to avoid punishment because of the boy's murder.

Although Betzinez's account should have settled the

McComas story for all time, whispers and rumors have continued to echo down through the years. Obviously people like to hold tightly to their myths and legends.

CRITTERS IN COURT

Sometimes it's difficult not to laugh at the antics of our fellow humans. They can be particularly foolish when they exercise their wisdom in the matter of applying the law. Did you know that during the middle ages it was not uncommon for animals to be taken to court to answer for their crimes?

Actually the practice of punishing animals for breaking the law is as old as the Bible. According to the Book of Exodus, "When an ox gores a man or a woman to death, the ox shall be stoned."

The majority of records concerning animal trials come to us from the middle ages, with serious questions concerning the veracity of some of the stories. Medieval scholars were well known for failing to provide explicit information about their sources. We know without a doubt some of the tales were either made up or were textbook cases fabricated as a way to keep law students from falling asleep. I believe the cases included here are well enough documented that we can accept them as mostly true. I'm not smart enough to make this stuff up.

The first recorded "animal trial" was held at Worms, Germany in 864 A.D. The Court declared a hive of bees that had stung a man to death should be suffocated.

Although all sorts of animals fell afoul of the medieval court system, it seems most of the animal offenders were pigs, at least in medieval France where pigs freely roamed the village streets. It was not uncommon to see a pig, perhaps dressed in human clothing and tied to a wheel, being publicly flogged for breaking the law. Flogging was reserved for fairly benign crimes. More serious crimes demanded more serious punishments. In 1394 one swine was tried for eating a child "although it was Friday." Eating meat on Fridays was a serious violation of church law that "was urged by the prosecuting attorney and accepted by the court as a serious aggravation of the porker's offense." The pig was found guilty and hung.

A sow and her six piglets were accused of a similar crime in 1547. The sow was executed, but her piglets were spared because of their youth and the bad example set by their mother.

In one, fairly typical 1379 case two herds of swine were feeding together when a trio of pigs became agitated, and charged the swine master's son, who died from his injuries. All of the pigs from both herds were tried, and "after due process of law, were condemned to death." All but the three instigating pigs were implicated as accomplices, and later pardoned. Records don't show just how the three convicted pigs were executed, though it was common for offending animals to be hanged or burned alive for their crimes.

All sorts of animals were tried throughout Europe. In 1471 in Basel, Switzerland, a chicken was tried by a court of law and found guilty of laying an egg "in defiance of natural law." The record doesn't explain how an egg can be laid in defiance of natural law, but the chicken was condemned to death and burned at the stake as "a devil in disguise."

Animal trials were normally conducted according to established legal procedures, and some lawyers made a reputation as defense counsels. The trial of a bear that had ravaged some German villages in 1499 was delayed for more than a week for legal arguments on a submission that the bear had a right to be judged by its peers—in this case a jury of fellow bears. No record survives as whether the court empanelled a jury of bears or whether the rogue bear was even actually tried.

Sometimes you have to wonder whether the lawyers and judges were actually serious or whether they were having a bit of fun with the system. A French lawyer, Bartholomew Chassenée, made a reputation with his skillful defense of some rats that had destroyed a barley crop in 1521. When the rats failed to appear for the trial, he successfully argued that the summons was invalid because it should have been served on all the rats in the district. When the new summons also was ignored, Chassenée pleaded that evilly disposed cats, belonging to the prosecutors, were intimidating the rats, and demanded a cash guarantee that the cats would not molest the rats on their way to court. The prosecution refused to give this guarantee, and the case was dismissed. Seriously, this really happened.

Trials of animals survived in Europe into the 20th Century. The most recent I discovered was in Switzerland in 1906. Two brothers and their dog were tried for murder. The two brothers were sentenced to life in prison. The poor dog must have been considered the ring-leader because it was condemned to death.

As barbaric, strange, or silly as animal trials may seem, in some places in the world they have continued well into the modern era. Here in 1916, in the American state of Tennessee, an elephant named Mary was convicted of murdering her trainer and was sentenced to be hung. Due to the size and weight of the condemned, a crane was used to carry out the sentence. The most recent case I found was in 1974 in Libya. A dog was tried for the crime of biting a human and sentenced to a month's imprisonment on a diet of bread and water. Justice was deemed to have been done when the dog served its sentence and was released.

Theoretically the more enlightened members of today's worldwide judicial system have determined animals cannot reason and therefore cannot actually commit a crime. If your dog happens to bite someone today, you're the one who'll get hauled into court.

DELINQUENT HERO

I'd like to introduce a young man you've most likely seen in movies or on television. You may have thought you knew him, without realizing he was actually a chaotic mixture of delinquent, real life hero, and a highly successful Hollywood star.

Terence Steven McQueen, born on March 24, 1930 in Beech Grove, Indiana, was nicknamed "The King of Cool" when he was a top box-office draw during the 1960s and 1970s. Not many realize his childhood was considerably less than ideal. His father, Terrence, was a stunt pilot and his mother, Julian, was an alleged alcoholic prostitute. His father abandoned Steve and his mother when he was only a few months old. Unable to cope with raising a child, Julian left little Steve in the care of his great-granduncle Claude Thompson on his Slater, Missouri farm.

In 1942 Steve's mother remarried, and reunited with 12 years old Steve in Los Angeles, California. The reunion didn't go well. His stepfather, when he was drunk, which was most of the time, beat Steve and his mother. Steve rebelled by taking to the streets where he got involved with local gangs. After he twice got caught stealing hubcaps his mother decided she couldn't handle the rebellious boy and sent him to reform school.

At the California Junior Boys' Republic in Chino McQueen frequently broke the rules, and even escaped several times. He eventually settled down under the guidance of a staff member. McQueen believed the experience at Boys' Republic changed his life. "I would have ended up in jail or something" Steve said. "I

21

was a wild kid,"

McQueen's mother never visited during his time at Boys' Republic and rarely wrote to him. Despite hard feelings toward his mother, the 16-year-old McQueen agreed to join her in New York City. However, when he discovered his mother had put him up in another apartment instead of letting him live with her, McQueen took off. Even though he was only sixteen, he managed to finagle a job aboard the SS *Alpha*. It may have been a dislike for being a merchant seaman, or it might have been his aversion to discipline, but he jumped ship while docked in the Dominican Republic.

Steve earned passage back to the United States by working as a towel boy in a brothel. Obviously McQueen's life was not headed in a positive direction. He was bitter, angry, and completely without purpose. Steve knew something had to change. As he explained, "It was all very pleasant just lying in the sun and watching the girls go by, but one day I suddenly felt bored so I went and joined the Marines."

He probably lied to enlist since he was only seventeen, and from his early service record, he was lucky he didn't end up with a BCD (Bad Conduct Discharge). After Boot Camp he was promoted to Private First Class and assigned to an amphibious tank unit. He tested the limits of the Marine Corps' sufferance which isn't known for its patience. McQueen was allegedly busted back to private seven times, but that's likely an exaggeration. Having been a Marine myself, it's hard to believe any Marine could be promoted and busted that many times in only a couple of years. His rebellious nature came to a head when he let a weekend pass turn into a two week tryst with his girlfriend. He resisted when the shore patrol apprehended him, and was sentenced to 41 days in the brig; the first 21 spent on bread and water. Perhaps his brig time gave Steve the opportunity to examine his attitude. Upon his release he attempted to improve himself and embody Marine values.

His chance at redemption came on a training exercise in the Arctic which turned disastrous. His ship hit a sandbank which threw several amphibious tanks and their crews into the water. Many drowned immediately, unable to get out of their vehicles, but several Marines were floundering in the icy water. McQueen couldn't just stand around watching his buddies drown. Without a thought for his own safety McQueen dove into the freezing water and began pulling anyone he could reach to safety. He managed to save five Marines before be was completely exhausted and had to be pulled from the water himself.

His heroic actions that day went a long way toward balancing the Marine Corps scales in his favor—but not enough to earn a meritorious citation. However, perhaps in recognition of his actions (or to keep him out of further trouble), McQueen was chosen to partake in the Honor Guard protecting Harry S. Truman's yacht.

McQueen was honorably discharged from the Marines in 1950. "The Marines gave me discipline I could live with. By the time I got out, I could deal with things on a more realistic level. All in all, despite my problems, I liked my time in the Marines," McQueen said.

As a civilian he took advantage of the G.I. Bill to study acting at Sanford Meisner's Neighborhood Playhouse. Most of you will remember Steve McQueen as an actor in television and movies. His first major role was on the TV series *"Wanted: Dead or Alive"* (1958 – 1961). His big Hollywood break came when Frank Sinatra hired him for the part of Bill Ringa in *Never So Few* (1959).

As the King of Cool he maintained his star status in 27 movies such as *The Magnificent Seven (1960), The Great Escape* (1963), *Bullitt* (1968), *The Thomas Crown Affair* (1968) and *The Getaway* (1972). His final two films, *Tom Horn* and *The Hunter* were both released in 1980.

McQueen suffered from mesothelioma and doctors warned him his heart might not withstand the surgery to remove multiple tumors in his neck and midsection. On November 7, 1980, hours after the tumors were removed, McQueen died of cardiac arrest.

JAMES R. OLSON

Very few know Steve McQueen began life as a juvenile delinquent who had the real life courage to brave freezing arctic waters and rescue five fellow Marines.

KING TO THE RESCUE

During May, 1842, Dick King, a young Englishman living in Natal, South Africa, made one of the longest endurance rides in recorded history, traveling by horseback 600 miles in 10 days.

During the 1840s there was a great deal of tension between the English and Boer settlers in South Africa. The Boers, also known as Afrikaners, were of Dutch or French Huguenot descent. This was the period of European expansion when several of the European powers were in the process of carving empires out of the African continent, without any consideration of the native population's rights.

Completely ignoring the claims of the warrior Zulu nation, who had been living in the region long before any Europeans had set foot in South Africa, the Boers and the English were prepared to fight each other for the right to exploit the lush lands of Natal.

In 1835 the British annexed the harbor of Port Natal, (now Durban) by sending a garrison of 250 English troops under the command of Captain Charlton Smith, to occupy the tiny village. In the meantime the Boers had consolidated their position inland, establishing the Republic of Natalia and were intent on expelling the British force from the strategic bay area.

This soon led to the Battle of Congella, where the English suffered heavy casualties, forcing the British garrison to retreat to their tented camp where their only defenses were trenches and earthworks. The camp was besieged by the Boers who kept up a small arms and artillery attack continuously, day after day.

Chivalrously, under a flag of truce, the Boers allowed the evacuation of the English women and children to a cargo ship in the bay.

Outnumbered six to one, the English forces were in serious danger of being annihilated. There was no way the small garrison could withstand the Boer attacks indefinitely, and the nearest relief forces were six hundred miles away in Grahamstown. More than likely the English would be killed or captured before the news of their plight even reached Grahamstown. Their only hope was to hold out until a courier on horseback could reach other British troops. Even under ideal circumstances the journey through thick jungle and over rugged mountains required at least seventeen days to complete. The most optimistic estimate placed relief six weeks away—if someone were even able to safely ride for help. Things were not looking good for the English.

Dick King, a 30 year old farmer, along with his sixteen year old servant boy Ndongeni, volunteered to ride for help. Because they needed to travel lightly, they carried a single pistol, two blankets, and a small supply of biscuits and biltong (biltong is a form of dried, cured meat that originated in Southern African countries, and is related to beef jerky since they are both spiced, dried meats).

With Captain Smith's blessing, and the prayers of the entire garrison, on the moonless night of May 23rd, King and Ndongeni, with their horses, managed to sneak past the Boer blockade to begin the dangerous journey to Grahamstown. Ahead lay more than one hundred crocodile infested rivers, the great and beautiful Drakensburg Mountains, and the territory of the fearsome Zulus. To remain unseen by the many enemies along the route, King chose to travel mostly at night and rest during the day.

Two hundred miles into the journey, Ndongeni's horse faltered and the servant boy was forced to turn back. Dick King continued alone until he was felled by a fever that incapacitated him for two days. Weak and weary, King pushed on and reached Grahamstown ten days after escaping Port Natal. A relief forced immediately began assembling the men and supplies needed to effect a rescue, knowing there was no time to waste.

On June 24th, one month after he began his attempt to reach help, and two weeks sooner than the most optimistic estimate, Dick King returned to Port Natal on the rescue ship *Conch*. Smith's garrison was only days away from either surrendering or starving.

In this modern age of air travel and super highways where speeds of seventy-five miles per hour are common, it's difficult to appreciate the magnitude of Dick King's ride. He was able to average seventy-five miles per day during a time when thirty-five miles per day was considered to be the upper limits of endurance. It is unlikely anyone, riding a single horse, will ever exceed Dick King's endurance ride.

The Boer War ended, as eventually do all wars, with the English victorious. As reward for their heroism, the native boy, Ndongeni received a farm at the Mzimkulu River. Dick King received a farm at Isipingo where he also managed a sugar mill until his death in 1871.

On August 14, 1915, a statue commemorating Dick King and his endurance ride was unveiled on the north shore of Durban Bay where it can be seen today.

QUEEN OF MAGIC

Although you may never have heard of Adelaide Herrmann, at the beginning of the 20th Century she was known throughout the world as The Queen of Magic. She was even more widely revered than her famous contemporary, Harry Houdini. Perhaps it's time for the world to know her again.

Adelaide Scarcez was born in London in 1853, and aspired to be a dancer. In 1875 she married Alexander Herrmann, a magician billed as Herrmann the Great. She began her magic career as assistant to her husband. Together, Alexander and Adelaide entertained audiences with thrilling magic tricks as they toured the United States, Mexico, South America, and Europe.

Alexander tragically died in 1896, when Adelaide was 43 years old. Even though Alexander had been successful and made a lot of money, it was not nearly enough to retire on. Adelaide also genuinely loved magic, and didn't want to stop. However, she was faced with a dilemma—an assistant was nothing without her magician.

She initially agreed to work with her husband's nephew, Leon Herrmann, who had worked mostly in Europe. However, Leon was not a very talented magician and a clash of personalities led them to a parting of the ways after only three seasons.

Without any money or any other means of supporting herself, Adelaide made the decision to carry on with her own magic act, even though there were no other female magicians at the time. She dove head-first into the magic industry and made a name for herself practically overnight. People loved her work.

She embraced her femininity and her own talents by show-casing them on stage in a way that audiences had never seen before. She called her show "Magic, Grace, and Music". She wore beautiful gowns, and danced during her magic acts. She hired other young dancers to join in the show, as well.

Adelaide Herrmann became extremely well-known as a magician in her own right, earning the moniker "The Queen of Magic." She toured as a headliner for over 25 years and performed internationally, touring London and Paris, and in 1903 made her Broadway debut. She performed often with other vaudeville acts and was frequently mentioned in the *New York Times.* In a November 2, 1899 article for Broadway Magazine entitled "The World's Only Woman Magician," Adelaide stated, "I shall not be content until I am recognized by the public as a leader in my profession, and entirely irrespective of the question of sex."

In order to be fully respected in the magic community, Adelaide had to do a trick that was hard for even men to pull off successfully. Right out of the gate, she performed the magic bullet trick during "Magic, Grace, and Music". Instead of just one person shooting at her, she would invite six men to fire their guns at her, and "catch" the bullets with her teeth. By doing such a gutsy magic trick, even all of the male magicians in the industry instantly respected her.

Her favorite illusion was "The Phantom Bride". Adelaide would hypnotize a female volunteer, cover her with a white silk cloth and levitate the volunteer "bride" on a brightly lit stage. She passed a hoop over her hovering form, showing there were no wires. When Adelaide pulled away the white silk cloth—the bride had disappeared—much to the amazement of the audience. As with all good magicians, Adelaide never revealed the secret of how the illusion was done.

In 1926, all the props from Adelaide Herrmann's magic act were destroyed when her storage buildings caught on fire and burned to the ground. She was in her 70's, and she lost absolutely everything. Despite this major setback, she decided to rebuild and start over from scratch. She created completely new acts with things she could pull together quickly. Audiences still loved her act, and were impressed that she was able to make a comeback.

Adelaide Herrmann performed her beloved magic right up until the day of her death of pneumonia on February 19, 1932. She is buried at the Woodlawn Cemetery, New York.

Since you've probably never heard of Adelaide Herrmann, you may honestly wonder, if the Queen of Magic was really so amazing, why isn't she remembered along side the likes of Harry Houdini? The simple answer is, I don't know. Certainly, if you believe the reports of contemporary artists and the adoring audiences, Adelaide was one of the all time great Magicians and deserves a place side by side with the all time greats. Perhaps her lack of fame has something to do with the warehouse fire that destroyed most of her belongings. One of the reason magicians like Houdini are remembered is because collectors played up his memory to make personal items and magic props seem extremely valuable. Without any financial motivation to keep her memory alive, everyone stopped talking about Adelaide Herrmann after a few years. If the fire had never happened, the world might still remember Adelaide Herrmann and pay her the respect she's due.

Unfortunately, the world of stage magic is still dominated by men. Perhaps very few young girls become magicians because they don't have female role models to look up to. But Adelaide proved over a hundred years ago that sometimes, being yourself and displaying your talent can pay off in a big way, and that girls can be magicians, too.

QUEEN VICTORIA, HEROINE

In fairy tales Princes and Princesses fall in love, marry, and live happily ever after. In real life it didn't always work out that way. Marriages were generally arranged for political purposes, to forge or strengthen ties between countries, without any consideration for the desires of the prospective bride or groom. Suitors were rated by whoever would forge the most advantageous union. However, England's feisty Queen Victoria had no intention of following political conventions. She was determined to marry for love.

Alexandrina Victoria was born on May 24, 1819, the only child of Edward, Duke of Kent, and Victoria Saxe-Saalfield-Coburg, sister of Leopold, king of the Belgians. When Alexandrina Victoria's father died in 1820, she became the heir apparent to the English throne at only 8 months old. Educated at the Royal Palace by a governess, she had a gift for drawing and painting and developed a passion for journal writing.

When King William IV died in June 1837, Alexandrina Victoria became Queen Victoria of England at the very young and tender age of 18.

It was not acceptable for the young Queen to remain unmarried. Victoria was well aware of the various political matrimonial plans being hatched by her court and counselors. As was her duty, she critically appraised a parade of eligible princes, still determined to marry for love.

Of all the suitors, she was attracted to Prince Albert of Saxe-Coburg and Gotha. About Albert, she made the following notation in her journal. "He is extremely handsome; his hair is about the same colour as mine; his eyes are large and blue, and he has a beautiful nose and a very sweet mouth with fine teeth; but the charm of his countenance is his expression, which is most delightful." Apparently the attraction was mutual.

Since Victoria was queen, Albert couldn't propose to her, so she proposed to him on October 15, 1839. They were married on February 10, 1840. Initially Albert was not popular with the British public. He was perceived to be from an impoverished and undistinguished minor state, barely larger than a small English county. However when the devotion between Queen and Prince Consort became obvious the public took him to heart.

On February 9, 1841 the young couple went for a walk on the freezing grounds of Buckingham Palace. It was only a day before their first wedding anniversary—a date which had also been chosen for the christening of their first-born child Princess Vicky.

They had managed to shake off most of their attendants. The Queen had one Maid of Honor with her, but Prince Albert had left the palace without telling anyone. Apparently Albert, an avid sportsman who loved to skate and play hockey, had carried along his ice skates. When the couple reached the frozen lake, he strapped on his skates and headed out onto the ice, while Victoria and her maid watched the Prince from shore. As the future queen, she had never learned to skate, since she had never been allowed to participate in dangerous activities.

Albert made a circuit of the ice covered lake and was returning to Victoria when the ice gave way and he was suddenly immersed in the freezing water. Queens, who are constantly surrounded by attendants, are not prepared to act as life savers. Yet realizing there was no one else to help, and that Albert's was in mortal danger, Victoria remained calm and reacted coolly. With her maid holding the Queen's left hand and acting as an anchor, Victoria reached out with her right hand and grasped

Albert's arm pulling him toward shore. Although Albert had a cut on his chin and was on the verge of hypothermia, Victoria's cool courage had saved his life. He returned home, took a hot bath and a nap, and was up a few hours later to socialize when their uncle Leopold (Victoria and Albert were first cousins) came to visit.

Had Albert died that day on the ice, it could have completely changed European history. Victoria and Albert already had a daughter, and the future King Edward VII was probably conceived around this time. If Albert had died, seven of Victoria's children wouldn't have been born—children who were married to nobles and rulers across Europe (during World War I, seven of their direct descendants were on thrones as king or queen). And if the future Edward VII hadn't been conceived, and Albert died, and everything else remained the same, it's possible Kaiser Wilhelm II may have become the ruler of both Germany and the United Kingdom.

On December 9, 1861, one of Albert's doctors diagnosed him with typhoid fever. After a brief illness, Albert died at 10:50 p.m. on December 14, 1861 at Windsor Castle. After Albert's death, Victoria plunged into deep mourning and avoided public appearances.

Victoria never remarried and continued her reign for 40 years until her death. She died on Tuesday, January 22, 1901, at the age of 81. Her son and successor, King Edward VII, and her eldest grandson, Emperor Wilhelm II, were at her deathbed.

Queen Victoria achieved many epic marks in history, but it's likely none of them would have happened if she hadn't first saved her husband from drowning.

RAGS, A WAR HERO

If you ever visit the Aspen Hill Pet Cemetery in Silver Spring, Maryland please visit the granite grave stone with the inscription, "Rags, War Hero, 1st Division Mascot WW I." This is the story of the animal buried there—Rags, a derelict puppy about whom at least three books, including one for children, have been written.

On July 14, 1918, World War I was in its final year when an American soldier, Private James Donovan, was on a stroll through the streets of Paris. He was enjoying the last few minutes of an all too brief break before he had to return to his unit, the 1st Infantry Division, and the war.

Donovan saw what he thought was a bundle of rags lying in a doorway, and would have passed without a second thought except he noticed the bundle moving. To his surprise, the rags turned out to be an emaciated mixed breed terrier puppy. An immediate bond was forged when Donovan gave the starving pup food and water and the loving attention all dogs crave.

Because he had taken the time to feed the puppy, Private Donovan was already late in returning to the base. He hated the thought of abandoning the dog again, but regulations strictly forbid soldiers having pets. He needn't have worried. There was no way of discouraging the dog from following him wherever he went, which included following him to his base. To avoid punishment for being late Donovan picked up the puppy and explained to the Military Police he was late because he had been out searching for the Division's mascot—Rags. The ruse worked, and Rags unofficially became the Division's mascot.

When Donovan's unit was transferred to the front lines, he left Rags behind with the headquarters staff where he would be safe. However, Rags didn't want to be safe. He wanted to be with Donovan. He escaped his make shift kennel and made his way across the war torn countryside until he joyfully found Donovan in the forward trenches. All the men in Donovan's unit were so happy to see Rags no effort was made to send him back to safety.

Voice communication between the front lines and headquarters was sporadic because the telephone lines, which were laid on the ground, were frequently cut by exploding shells. When that happened, soldiers were tasked with the extremely dangerous job of running messages back and forth. The Germans delighted in chasing the messengers with rifle and machine gun fire. Because Rags seemed able to find his way around, Donovan quickly trained him to carry messages back to headquarters when telephone communication was out. Obviously Rags was smaller and quicker than any human, and had an inherent skill at dodging gunfire and getting through obstacles such as barbed wire while delivering messages.

Rags quickly demonstrated he had many more talents than being a courier. He also had a knack for quickly finding breaks in the telephone lines, and leading repair crews to fix them.

When Rags first came to the trenches he noticed the soldiers would hit the ground when they heard the sound of an incoming mortar attack so he started to do the same. In fact, with his keen sense of hearing Rags soon became the first to hit the ground. The men quickly learned if Rags went down so did they. Those early warnings saved many lives.

The front line trenches were always a dangerous place, but on October 9, 1918 the Germans launched the bloody Meuse-Argonne offensive which was the last major battle of World War I. Until this point, both Rags and Private Donovan had survived with no major injuries. A German artillery barrage during this last battle would change that.

Rags suffered leg injuries, was blinded in one eye, lost hearing in one ear and was mildly gassed. Donovan was far more seriously wounded and badly gassed. Rags healed rather quickly but Donovan was not so fortunate. His injuries eventually required his return to the States, and a sojourn in the hospital at Fort Sheridan, just outside Chicago. Knowing how important Rags was to Donovan, men of his unit smuggled the puppy aboard the ship taking Donovan back to the U.S.

At Fort Sheridan Rags lived in the base firehouse and visited Donovan daily in his hospital room. Even the best care wasn't enough for the badly injured young soldier. In early 1919 Donovan died from his wounds. An inconsolable Rags continued living at the firehouse where the soldiers cared for him.

In 1920 Rags found a forever home with Major Raymond Hardenbergh, his wife and two daughters, who had fallen in love with the terrier. As with all military families, the Hardenberghs moved frequently and Rags became popular at each base where the Major was posted. When stationed in New York, the Army press released a story about the dog's heroic acts during the war and Rags became a well-loved celebrity. In 1928 he proudly marched down Broadway with the 1st Division troops as part of the 10th anniversary of the end of the War to end all wars.

In March 1936 Rags, believed to be 20 years old, died peacefully in his sleep. Many of the soldiers he had served beside were in attendance as Rags was buried with full military honors at the Aspen Hill Pet Cemetery in Silver Spring, Maryland.

Not all heroes walked on two legs.

received in combat.

Although his birth certificate claims William Henry Johnson was born in Winston-Salem, North Carolina, no one is quite sure when. The official U.S. Army website honoring Johnson's service lists an approximate birth date of July 15, 1892. Other research indicates he could have been born as early as 1887 or as late as 1897.

He was living in Albany, New York, working either in a coal yard or as a railway porter, when he opened a newspaper in the spring of 1917 and read that the 15th New York Infantry Regiment of the New York National Guard was accepting enlistees. The regiment was comprised entirely of black soldiers.

Johnson showed up at the recruiting office on June 5, 1917, weighing a slight 130 pounds and standing 5 feet, 4 inches tall. He was so small the recruiter briefly questioned if he was old enough to be a soldier. Johnson was shipped to France on January 1, 1918.

The wounds he's received in France probably shortened Johnson's life because he died of heart failure on July 1, 1929, age about 37.

At some point after his death people became interested in William Henry Johnson gaining some of the recognition his country owed him. In 1996 he was awarded a posthumous Purple Heart, the medal recognizing his wounds in combat. There apparently was some doubt about where he had been buried, but historians determined Johnson had been buried at Arlington National Cemetery. With confirmation of the gravesite, in 2002 Johnson was awarded the Army's second highest award for valor, the Distinguished Service Cross.

In 2015, William Henry Johnson was posthumously awarded the Medal of Honor, which was accepted on Johnson's behalf by Sergeant Major Louis Wilson of the New York National Guard. And every June 5, Albany celebrates Henry Johnson Day in acknowledgement of the day he enlisted.

Although it was nearly a hundred years too late, Sergeant Johnson finally received the recognition he deserved.

SOME INTERESTING FACTS

Join me in checking out some interesting facts you probably never knew.

Johnny Appleseed

Most people think of Johnny Appleseed as a mythical figure much like Paul Bunyan and Babe, his pet blue ox. However, Johnny Appleseed actually existed. His real name was John Chapman (1774 – 1845), who was an American pioneer nurseryman who introduced apple trees to large parts of Pennsylvania, Ohio, Indiana, and Illinois, as well as the northern counties of present-day West Virginia. He became an American legend while still alive, due to his kind, generous ways, his leadership in conservation, and the symbolic importance he attributed to apples. But the apples on the trees Johnny planted were not the tasty fruits you'd find in the supermarket today. Johnny Appleseed's apples were actually bitter in taste because he didn't expect his fruits to be eaten whole, but rather made into hard apple cider.

Kleenex

One weapon used by both sides of World War I was poisonous gas, which prompted both sides to issue gas masks to their combat troops. An important ingredient of the gas mask filters was cotton, and when there was a cotton shortage a substitute for cotton needed to be found. Kimberly-Clark, a large paper company located in Neenah, Wisconsin, worked to develop a thin, flat, paper substitute for cotton the army could use as a filter in gas masks. The war ended before scientists perfected the material, so Kimberly-Clark redeveloped it to be smoother and softer, and marketed it to the public as Kleenex. The product originally intended as a filter in gas masks, became so popular that Kleenex has become synonymous with facial tissue.

Our Fifty Star Flag

In 1958, for an American history project during his junior year of high school, Bob Heft designed a 50-star flag. At the time there were only 48 states, but Bob had a hunch two more states would soon be added. Bob's teacher was unimpressed and gave him a B- asking if he even knew how many states we had, and telling him, "If you don't like the grade, get your flag accepted in Washington then come back and see me." In 1959, Alaska and Hawaii became our 49th and 50th states and Bob sent his flag design to Washington. Two years later he received a call from President Dwight D. Eisenhower who invited him to Washington, D.C., for a ceremony adopting his 50-star flag. Bob's teacher also went back and changed his grade to an A. Betsy Ross may have designed the first American flag, but the flag currently representing our country was designed by a high school student.

The Poisonous Fruit

Many scholars believe Hernán Cortés, the Spanish explorer, brought tomato seeds from the New World in 1519 with the intent of the fruits being used ornamentally in gardens. By the 1700s, aristocrats had begun eating tomatoes. Tomatoes soon became known as the "poison apple" because the aristocrats got sick and died after eating them. The truth was that wealthy Europeans used pewter plates, which were high in lead content. Because tomatoes are so highly acidic, they leached lead from the plates, resulting in many deaths from lead poisoning. Since no one made the connection between plate and poison at the time, the tomato was identified as the culprit. Tomatoes were shunned for nearly a hundred years until around 1880, with the invention of the pizza in Naples, Italy. Soon the tomato grew widespread in popularity in Europe and the rest of the world.

The Microwave Oven

Between 1937 and 1940, British physicist Sir John Turton Randall, together with a team of British coworkers, developed the multi-cavity magnetron which allowed for production of electromagnetic waves of a small enough wavelength (microwaves) to develop radar. Magnetron technology was given to the U.S. government in September 1940 in exchange for their financial and industrial help during the Second World War. One of the companies that were given contracts by the U.S. government to build magnetrons was Raytheon. One of the engineers working for Raytheon was self-taught engineer Percy Spencer. He was at that time one of the world's leading experts in radar tube design. In 1945 he noticed a radar set using electromagnetic waves melted the candy bar in his pocket. He had the idea to make a metal box using microwaves to heat food. Raytheon filed for the patent because Spencer was an employee and all of his work was done in the name of the company. Although Percy Spenser never received any royalties from his invention, he wasn't forgotten. His reward for inventing an appliance used in nearly every American household was a $2 bonus.

Man vs Horse

Have you ever seen one of those old Western movies where the hero escapes the posse by having his horse leap an impossible distance across a gap between sheer cliffs? Or have you seen the adventure movies where the hero leaps across the gap between two tall buildings, only to barely make it, clinging on by his finger tips? Then with nothing better to do with your time, have you wondered which could make the longer jump, man or horse? You might be surprised to learn the Olympic world record for the longest human long jump is greater than the world record for longest horse long jump. Mike Powell set the record in 1991 by jumping 29.36 feet, and the horse Extra Dry set the record in 1900 by jumping 20.01 feet. Just think, next time the question comes up in casual conversation you'll have the answer.

The World's Greatest Empire

There have been a number of large empires over the course of recorded history, but which was the greatest of all time? Was it Alexander the Great's conquered territory, or the mighty Roman Empire, or the conquests of Genghis Khan? According to the World Atlas, an empire "is a group of nations or people that are under the rule of a powerful government or an emperor of a territory usually larger than a kingdom." Under that definition, the British Empire was the greatest empire in history. At it's height in the 1920s Britain ruled over 23 percent of the world's population. That equates to about 13 million square miles. Just think how much larger it would have been if its American colony hadn't decided to go its own way.

Irish St. Patrick's Day

Every one is Irish on March 17th, St. Paddy's Day. Although St. Patrick's Day is a religious holy day, you might associate the day with green beer, wearing of the green and perhaps drinking so much you think you actually see leprechauns. However, until 1961, there were laws in Ireland that banned bars from being open on March 17th. Since the holy day falls during the period of Lent in the heavily Catholic country, the idea of binge drinking seemed a bit immoral. History tells us many Irish immigrated to America because of the great potato famine. Do you think it might actually have been because they couldn't have a green beer in Ireland on St. Paddy's Day?

No Letter A

It's fairly common knowledge that "E" is the most frequently used letter in the English language. Maybe less well known is that "A" is the second most frequently used letter. However, if you spell out the numbers, no number before 1,000 contains the letter A. If you don't want to take my word for it, you can spend the next few hours spelling out the numbers. You won't find any "A's", but there are plenty of, I's, O's, and U's.

I know you'll all sleep better tonight knowing these interesting facts. Pleasant dreams.

THE BUTTER LADY

Americans are known for their ingenuity during difficult times, but Caroline Brooks not only solved her family's financial problems, but became famous because of her solution.

She was born Caroline Shawk on April 28, 1840 in Cincinnati, Ohio. In 1862 she married railroad worker Samuel H. Brooks. The couple moved to Memphis, Tennessee, where Samuel's railroad job was located, but Samuel dreamed of being a farmer. In 1866 they relocated to a farm near Helena, in Phillips County, Arkansas.

The weather in 1867 proved disastrous for Samuel's cotton crop. He was barely able to salvage enough to feed their growing family. Farm women of the time often sold butter to supplement the family income. In order to differentiate one woman's butter from another's, the butter was formed in decoratively shaped molds. However, Caroline had always exhibited a talent for art, so rather than molding her butter, she sculpted the butter into shapes such as shells, animals, and faces. Since there was no money for traditional sculpting tools, she used "common butter-paddles, cedar sticks, broom straws and camel's-hair pencils". Her customers appreciated the skillfully sculpted butter, and there was a good market for her works.

Even when the cotton crops came in and the family's financial outlook improved, Caroline continued sculpting butter because her customers were willing to pay higher prices for the beautiful dairy products. During the long winter months Caroline began to be more creative in her butter sculptures. She loved the Greek myth of *Iolanthe*, mythological sea nymph and daughter of Oceanus. So she created a butter sculpture, *Dreaming Iolanthe*, depicting the beautiful girl.

This work was displayed in early 1874 at a Cincinnati gallery, to financial and critical success. During its two-week exhibition, about two thousand people paid admission to view it. An article appearing in *The New York Times* declared that the "translucence [of the butter] gives to the complexion a richness beyond alabaster and a softness and smoothness that are very striking", and that "no other American sculptress has made a face of such angelic gentleness as that of Iolanthe."

Butter is a delicate medium for a sculptress. If you've ever left the butter out on the dinning table you soon discovered it melted. Since there was no refrigeration in the 1870's, Caroline had to find some method to prolong the life of her sculptures. To preserve her delicate butter sculptures, she created them in flat metallic milk pans which she set in larger pans filled with ice. By continuing to supply the outer pans with ice, she was able to keep her butter sculptures in good condition for months.

Caroline created a version of *Iolanthe*, which was exhibited at the Centennial Exposition – the 1876 world's fair held in Philadelphia, Pennsylvania. Her butter sculpture, in the Women's Pavilion, attracted such large crowds Caroline was invited to move from the Women's Pavilion to the main exhibit space. This was an honor, but there may have been an additional motivation behind the invitation. Many serious art patrons believed female artists in general didn't have the skill to actually create the works for which they were taking credit. As a demonstration that she had, in fact, sculpted the piece, she created another head, in about ninety minutes, for a panel which included Exposition officials and members of the press. Observers were impressed by how quickly, using crude instruments to sculpt in an unusual medium, Caroline created a beautiful work of art. One guidebook proclaimed *Dreaming Iolanthe* to be the "most beautiful and unique exhibit in the Centennial".

When Caroline was invited to display her works in Paris, she was faced with a unique set of challenges. Sailing from New York to France with a life-size butter sculpture, required her to secure passage on a ship with sufficient ice to preserve her work throughout the journey. In France she faced the challenge of finding a railroad car with enough ice to safely transport the piece from Le Havre to the final destination in Paris. Caroline safely completed the journey to the acclaim of the French art world.

Every artist, in whatever medium, desires their works to have some degree of permanence. After preserving her original butter *Dreaming Iolanthe* for a half a year, Caroline desired a method which would not require keeping it in cold storage. Without knowing ahead of time what the results may be, she mixed up some plaster and poured it onto the butter sculpture. The plaster quickly set, and she cut a hole in the bottom of the milk pan which held her creation. Brooks then set the pan over a container of boiling water, and the melted butter drained out of the hole. She removed the remainder of the bottom of the pan, and was left with a greased plaster negative. She placed more plaster inside and, after some difficulty removing the outer layer, was left with a successful plaster positive. Brooks was issued a patent in 1877 for her process of creating lubricated plaster molds

She died in St. Louis in 1913. Very little of her work survives in public collections, but she is remembered not only as the "Centennial Butter Sculptress", but also as a feminist pioneer.

THE FIRST LADY DOCTOR

When Elizabeth was twenty-four, her good friend suffering from a terminal disease, confessed to Elizabeth she felt embarrassed going to male doctors. She believed she would have fared better having a female physician. Unfortunately there was not a single female physician in the entire country. That's when Elizabeth decided she wanted to be a doctor.

Elizabeth Blackwell was born on February 3, 1821 in Bristol, England. In 1832, the Blackwell family moved to the United States, first settling in New York and later moving to Cincinnati, Ohio. In August 1838, Elizabeth's father died of fever, leaving the family nearly destitute.

With the family's survival at stake, Elizabeth, age 17, and her older sisters Anna and Marian started a school in their home. The Cincinnati English & French Academy for Young Ladies made enough money to keep the family going until the youngest children reached maturity.

It was at this point Elizabeth decided to pursue a career in medicine. But the road to becoming a doctor was not an easy one. Not only were there no female doctors in America at the time, but no medical schools were interested in having female students. While she began sending applications to every medical school in the United States, Elizabeth worked as a medical assistant in doctor's offices.

In October 1847, the Geneva Medical College—the thirtieth

application she had sent out—sent her a letter of acceptance. Unknown to Elizabeth, when her application arrived at Geneva Medical College, there was a serious debate whether the school should accept the application. To solve the debate the administration asked the students to decide whether or not to admit her. The students, reportedly believing the application to be a practical joke sent from a neighboring college, endorsed her admission.

When a real live female showed up at the college in the town of Geneva, New York, there was a community and student uproar due to the prejudices over women receiving a formal medical education. Elizabeth was ostracized by educators and patients alike. At first, she was even kept from classroom medical demonstrations, as inappropriate for a woman. Elizabeth held firm despite all the challenges, thereby earning the respect of most of her peers. It was also reported that uncouth male students became particularly studious and mature in her presence. It certainly helped that Elizabeth was easy to look at. Eventually writing her doctoral thesis on typhus fever she graduated first in her 1849 class, becoming the first woman to become a doctor of medicine in the United States.

Elizabeth wasn't satisfied with just being a doctor. She wanted to become a surgeon, which would require further study. After becoming a naturalized United States citizen, she left for Europe, working in London and Paris. She was working in midwifery at La Maternité in Paris when her hopes of becoming a surgeon were doomed forever. She was treating an infant when pus from a wound accidentally squirted into Elizabeth's left eye. The eye became infected and she lost the sight in that eye.

In 1851 Elizabeth Blackwell returned to New York, where hospitals and dispensaries uniformly refused her affiliation. She was even refused lodging and office space by landlords when she sought to set up a private practice. She had to purchase a house in which to begin her practice.

Having decided to avoid marriage, Elizabeth Blackwell

nevertheless sought a family, and in 1854 adopted an orphan, Katharine Barry, known as Kitty. They remained companions into Elizabeth's old age. "The utter loneliness of life became intolerable, and in October of 1854 I adopted a little orphan girl. Who will ever guess the restorative support which that poor little orphan has been to me? It was a dark time, and she did me good—her genial, loyal, Irish temperament suited me."

In the mid-1850s, she also opened a clinic in her home that became known as the New York Dispensary for Poor Women and Children. With help from her sister and fellow doctor Emily Blackwell and physician Marie Zakrzewska, Elizabeth also established the New York Infirmary for Indigent Women and Children in 1857, an institution that would last for more than a century.

During the Civil War, the Blackwell sisters helped to organize the Women's Central Association of Relief, selecting and training nurses for service in the war. Having maintained that clean, sanitary conditions were an important aspect of health, especially in war, Elizabeth helped establish the U.S. Sanitary Commission in 1861 under the auspices of President Abraham Lincoln.

Soon after the war Elizabeth returned to England. She set up a private practice and served as a lecturer at the London School of Medicine for Women. While lecturing in England, she became the first woman listed on the British Medical Register.

Elizabeth Blackwell had a profound impact on the progress of women in medicine. Together with her sister Emily, she opened the New York Infirmary for Women. She also traveled throughout the United States and England, lecturing on the subject of women in medicine. In her lifetime she personally influenced hundreds of women to enter the medical profession. Along with Florence Nightingale, she worked during the Civil War to organize nursing care for the wounded and, with Nightingale and others, opened the first medical school for women in England.

Elizabeth Blackwell died at her home in Hastings, England

on May 31, 1910. She was a grand visionary who opened the horizons for all women.

THE MAN WHO FOUND HIS OWN TOMBSTONE

Arguably one of the most famous Wild West mining towns, Tombstone, Arizona, is probably best remembered not for its mineral resources, but as the site of the gunfight at the OK Corral. Yet, Tombstone was the richest silver strike in America. About $85,000,000 in silver was produced from the mines in and around the boom town (about $2.37 billion in today's money). However, in popular history the man who discovered this vast wealth has been overshadowed by Wyatt Earp, Doc Holiday, and the other participants in the gunfight.

Edward Lawrence Schieffelin was born in 1847 in a coal-mining region of Wellsboro, Pennsylvania, the son of a prominent Pennsylvania family. In the mid-1850s the family relocated to the Rogue Valley, Oregon Territory, to raise cattle, grain and children. Not wanting to be a rancher, at age 17, Schieffelin set out on his own to be a prospector, searching for gold and silver in the southwestern states.

An 1876 contemporary described Ed Schieffelin as "about the strangest specimen of human flesh I ever saw. He was 6 feet 2 inches tall and had black hair that hung several inches below his shoulder and a beard that had not been trimmed or combed for so long a time that it was a mass of unkempt knots and mats.

He wore clothing pieced and patched from deerskins, corduroy and flannel, and his hat was originally a slouch hat that had been pieced with rabbit skin until very little of the original felt remained."

Schieffelin had a hunch there were valuable mineral deposits in the hills east of the San Pedro River in Arizona. Everyone with a lick of sense warned Ed to stay away from that extremely dangerous area, which was only about 12 miles from the hostile Chiricahua Apache stronghold in the Dragoon Mountains. His friend and army scout Al Sieber warned him, "Better take your coffin with you; you'll find your tombstone there, and nothing else."

After many months working the hills and dodging Apaches, Ed found pieces of silver ore in a dry wash near a high plateau called Goose Flats. Schieffelin was convinced his hunch had panned out and he was sitting on a fortune of silver. However, Ed was nearly flat broke and couldn't afford to pay for the legal paperwork to file a mining claim. By offering a partnership, Schieffelin persuaded William Griffith to pay the fees, and fittingly registered his claim as "The Tombstone Mine"—a jibe at those who'd told him he'd only find his tombstone in that part of Arizona.

Griffin gave up any partnership claims when some local men examined the ore samples and pronounced them worthless. Ed wasn't discouraged. He had confidence his find was valuable. With only 30 cents in his pocket, Schieffelin set out to find his brother Al, whom he had not seen in four years.

Ed found his brother working at the McCracken Mine in Signal City, Arizona. Ed and Al approached the mine's assayer, Richard Gird, and asked him if he thought their ore samples were worth anything. Three days later, Gird told Ed that he valued the best of the ore samples at $2,000 a ton. Ed, Al and Richard Gird formed a partnership on the spot. They shook hands on their three-way deal, a gentlemen's agreement that was never put down on paper but resulted in millions of dollars of wealth for all three men.

The three partners returned to Cochise County despite reports of continued Apache raids and the murder of miners and ranchers in the area. Gird found Schieffelin's initial find of silver ore promising, but within a few weeks of mining the vein, Ed discovered it ended in a pinch about three feet deep. Al and Gird were despondent but Ed was optimistic, knowing he could find more ore deposits. A couple weeks later Ed found another sample of float ore that looked promising. Al told Ed he was a "lucky cuss," and that became the name of one of the richest mining claims in the Tombstone District. The ore samples assayed at $15,000 a ton. Ed shortly afterward identified another claim, the "Tough Nut" lode, rich in horn silver.

On March 5, 1879, U.S. Deputy Mineral Surveyor Solon M. Allis finished laying out a new town site on top of the Tough Nut mine. He named the boom town "Tombstone" in honor of Schieffelin's initial mining claim.

On June 17, 1879, Schieffelin showed up in Tucson driving an ore wagon carrying the first load of silver bullion valued at $18,744 (about $504,013 today).

Tombstone's mining heyday was relatively short. In the late 1880s, the silver mines reached the water table and the mines eventually filled with water (with plenty of silver out of reach in the flooded shafts). Tombstone's population faded, until tourism became its main attraction fueled mostly by the gunfight at the OK Corral which had occurred October 26, 1881.

Ed had accumulated millions in wealth as a result of the silver boom. He cleaned himself up and traveled to New York City, Chicago, Washington, D.C., and other cities, meeting many distinguished people. Ever restless, over the next 20 years Ed showed up at nearly every boom town in the West.

Ed realized he preferred the rugged life of a lonely prospector to the luxurious life of a millionaire. Searching for wealth was more satisfying than actually finding the mother lode. On May 12, 1897, while prospecting in the Canyonville, Oregon area Ed Schieffelin was found dead; face down on the floor of his isolated miner's cabin. The coroner ruled his death the result of a heart attack.

Ed Schieffelin left a will that directed he be buried at Tombstone, Arizona where his grave can be seen today. In the end he had found his tombstone in that desert, just as his friends had predicted.

THE SWORD IN
THE STONE

Tales of Camelot, King Arthur, and the Knights of the Round Table have held generations enthralled. One legend I've always enjoyed is the one about the Sword in the Stone. Although it's been told with some contradictory details, the gist of the tale goes something like this. One morning a stone appears in London's market square. Embedded in the stone is a knight's sword with this message engraved on the visible portion of the blade: *"Whoever pulls out this sword from this stone is the true king of England!"*

The biggest and strongest men, noble and peasant alike, came from all parts of the kingdom and attempted to pull the sword from the stone. No matter how much these men struggled and strained, none were able to withdraw the sword. Finally a sixteen year old boy named Arthur stepped up to the sword and drew it from the rock as if it had been stuck in butter. Some variations of the legend claim this was Arthur's legendary sword Excalibur. Whether or not it was Excalibur, pulling the sword from the stone began the legend of King Arthur.

Although it's unlikely a young Arthur actually pulled a sword from a stone, legends do often have a basis in reality. In the real world a sword embedded in stone does actually exist. As far as I know, no one pulled this sword from the stone and went on to become a king. In fact, this sword is still stuck in its stone. This stone and sword are in Italy and have absolutely nothing to do with England or King Arthur. They are located at Monte Siepi Chapel in the San Galgano Abbey in Tuscany.

The sword in this legend allegedly belonged to San (Saint) Galgano Guidotti, who was born in 1148. Guidotti was an Italian knight as far removed from the chivalrous knights of Arthur's Round Table as it's possible to imagine. Galgano Guidotti, the son of a minor noble, was what Arthur's court would have called a black knight—a brutal and cruel knight constantly looking for trouble and worldly pleasures. One day, when Guidotti was 32, the Archangel Michael appeared to him, telling him he must end his life of sin and showed him the way to salvation. According to the legend, on that day Galgano Guidotti turned his life around and become a saint. Well, maybe not quite yet.

Legends always make change seem easy, but in real life it's much more difficult. Galgano Guidotti did not immediately do as the Archangel Michael suggested and commit to God. However he was out riding one day, most likely looking for mischief of some kind, when he came to Monte Siepi. Monte Siepi was just a hill with some bedrock in it, not yet including the impressive abbey and chapel that grace the landscape today. Something—a voice from Heaven, perhaps—told him again that he had to change his ways. He replied that it would be as difficult as "splitting rock with a sword." He then tried to demonstrate the hopelessness of his situation, but instead of breaking, his sword went straight into the rock. The story goes that Galgano used the rock with the sword in it as an altar for praying from that day forth, until he died roughly a year later.

Galgano Guidotti was canonized by Pope Lucius III in 1185. Starting on the year of his canonization, monks built a chapel around his sword and stone altar. Today, it overlooks the ruins of San Galgano Abbey from its site on the hill. The chapel still contains the sword in the stone, though it is now encased in plastic so people will not try to steal it, break it or become King of England with it. Legend has it that one fellow was set upon by a pack of wolves when he tried to take the sword. There is a pair of mummified hands in the chapel, which supposedly belonged to the thief.

For centuries, the sword was believed to be a fake by everyone except the most devout. The sword (or at least what can be seen of it) is a rather basic sword in a style typical for the 12th century. In 2001, metal analysis of the Guidotti sword revealed the weapon is very old, and there's nothing that supports the opinion of the sword being a recent fake.

For my part, I'd be more interested in how a 12th century sword could become seamlessly embedded up to its hilt in the bedrock. I'd be inclined to go along with the legend's description of how it came to be in the rock, since even the experts don't have a better explanation.

While the sword may never have belonged to Saint Galgano Guidotti (this is still not entirely certain), one thing is certain, it dates from around his lifetime. If it did not belong to him, it belonged to someone else of his era. The mummified hands are from around that time as well. There might even be some truth to the 800 year old legend of San Galgano's sword in the stone —even though it isn't quite as much fun (or well known) as the King Arthur legend.

THE UNSUNG HERO

The American Revolution's famous battles and heroes are well known by every school child. However, the only female heroine that comes readily to mind would be Betsy Ross, who may or may not have actually made the first American flag. This is the story of a virtually unknown skirmish—the Battle of Whitemarsh—which was the last major military engagement of 1777 between the British Army and the American rebels. Behind the victory of General George Washington and his men is a little known, unsung hero: Irish-American Quaker, Lydia Darragh. Only a dedicated historian would appreciate the significance of Washington's victory at Whitemarsh and Lydian Darragh's contribution.

Lydia Barrington Darragh was a Quaker, born in 1729 in Dublin, Ireland. Lydia married family friend William Darragh in 1753, and a few years later, the couple moved to America, settling in Philadelphia with its large Quaker community.

Although Philadelphia was a rebel hotbed, and the Darragh family's loyalties leaned toward the rebel cause, they were not directly involved in the war until 1777. In September of 1777, after several victories over Washington's army, the British marched triumphantly into Philadelphia. When Washington's October bid to retake the city failed, he and his troops retreated to Whitemarsh.

There were no British troops quartered in the Darragh house, although General Howe demanded use of the Darragh's home for meetings. One of the many British regulations the

American colonists protested was the quartering of uninvited British troops in colonial homes. William Darragh—aided by a cousin in the British army—persuaded the British to allow his family to stay in their home, although the youngest children were sent to relatives outside the city.

As well-known Quakers, the Darraghs felt relatively safe remaining in their home although British General Sir William Howe established his headquarters across the street from the Darraghs' house. Lydia took advantage of the proximity to the British headquarters, using her fourteen-year-old son John to smuggle coded notes about British activities to her eldest son Charles, a Patriot soldier.

On the night of December 2, 1777, General Howe and other officers commandeered one of her rooms for a secret conference. Although the family was ordered to stay in their bedrooms, Lydia hid in a closet where she overheard their plans for a surprise December 4th attack on Washington's army at Whitemarsh, 8 miles away. On the evening of December 4th, the British would advance toward Whitemarsh with 5,000 men, 13 cannons, and 11 boats on wheels.

Lydia realized a surprise December attack on the colonial army would be disastrous. Washington's troops were weary, hungry, and poorly supplied. It's likely the British would have crushed Washington's feeble army and ended the rebellion before Christmas. She was determined to warn General Washington, no matter the danger to herself, although she must have been aware that the young patriot, Nathan Hale, had been executed for spying just a year earlier.

Lydia used her role as homemaker to receive a pass from General Howe to visit her children and obtain flour from the Frankford mill. On December 4th, Lydia made the long and dangerous walk past patrol stops to the mill. She filled her flour sack and journeyed toward the Rising Sun Tavern, a known Patriot message center. She gave an American officer she recognized the message about Howe's planned attack, and then, securing her flour, hurried home.

Darragh's bravery gave Washington time to prepare his troops to ambush the British force. After four days of minimal fighting in what was ultimately a standoff, Howe and his troops returned to Philadelphia. Washington's army withdrew to winter quarters at Valley Forge, 22 miles northwest of Philadelphia.

Later, after the failed offensive, Major Andre, the British spymaster, would report, "One thing is certain, the enemy had notice of our coming, were prepared for us, and we marched back like a parcel of fools."

The British began an investigation into who leaked their plan. Of course everyone in the Darragh family was questioned, but officers believed Lydia's claims that no one knew what was discussed because they had all been asleep during the soldiers' secret meeting.

In June of 1778, the British abandoned Philadelphia and the fighting moved elsewhere in the colonies. Lydia Darragh's husband William died in June 1783, only three months before the Treaty of Paris officially ended the war. Three years later, Lydia moved into a new house and ran a store until her death in 1789. She never received any recognition for her contribution to the American cause.

Lydia Darragh was one of the many heroes of the Revolutionary War who has vanished into obscure history. Yet without her bravery and determination, the rebellion would've lost many lives at Whitemarsh and there is the very real possibility the colonies may have lost the war.

TWO ARIZONA CITIES

While researching my first novel I discovered these two tales of the founding and naming of two Arizona cities. As these stories unfold, see if you can guess the names these cities are known by today.

Arizona City

In the 21st Century the mighty Colorado River is no longer mighty. Millions of gallons of precious water have been diverted to provide drinking water for cities in Arizona and California, and even more millions of gallons for irrigation. It would not be a very challenging feat to wade across the river near the border between Arizona and Mexico.

In 1854 the river was completely different. High, spring time flood waters, the danger of quicksand and treacherous currents prevented travelers from attempting to ford the river. Consequently, an enterprising man named L.J. Jaeger had established a ferry to transport horses, wagons and people across the river on their journey to San Diego. Charles D. Posten and Herman Ehrenburg, returning to San Diego from a prospecting and surveying trip in Arizona, discovered they didn't have enough money to pay the ferry toll across the Colorado River for themselves and their stock. After having dodged Apaches all winter, the two men were determined not to allow a $25 fare to prevent them from reaching San Diego. Unpacking their equipment, Posten and Ehrenburg began to survey a town site on the east bank of the river.

Overcome by curiosity, Jaeger, the ferryman, came across the river to see what they were doing. Posten explained they were surveying the lots and streets of a new city, which they were going to register in San Diego. Some fast talking convinced Jaeger that by purchasing lots along the river bank, he would assure himself a monopoly on the ferry rights.

Although Posten and Ehrenburg had surveyed the town site as a ruse to obtain passage across the Colorado, they decided to actually register the site, which they named Arizona City. In 1873, the residents of Arizona City decided to rename their community after the local Indian tribe, becoming Yuma, Arizona.

Pumpkinville

By any definition, John W. (Jack) Swilling, was a larger than life figure in Arizona history. We know for certain he was an Indian fighter, prospector, ex-confederate officer, saloon owner, and a well known pioneer. Some of the stories surrounding him are a bit suspect because he had a tendency to tell wild tales while drinking or under the influence of narcotics, which he used to relieve the pain caused by old injuries. His friends, of which there were many, remembered Jack as an honest, hardworking, and generous man always ready to help those in need of a meal or a place to sleep. He was known to put his own life at risk for others, literally riding to the rescue when help was needed in the face of Apache attacks.

Perhaps he is best known as the Father of the Salt River Valley. Although others had noticed patterns of symmetrical, regular depressions in the desolate Salt River Valley, Swilling was the only one to do something about it. He was convinced the depressions were the remains of irrigation canals built by a pre-historic Indian civilization. Jack felt confident if Indians had been able to make the arid regions of central Arizona productive through irrigation, he could also. In September, 1867, he formed the Swilling Irrigating Canal Company, and immediately set to work clearing the accumulation of debris from centuries of neglect in the old Indian ditches. In March, 1868, the new flood gates were opened and precious water from the Salt River again flowed into the barren desert.

The settlement that flourished along the banks of the canals was named Pumpkinville in honor of the first modern crop grown in the desert. Understandably proud of his canals, Jack Swilling was unhappy with the commonplace name given to the new town. During a meeting of the leading citizens, Darrel Duppa, an educated Englishman and good friend of Swilling's, suggested since Pumpkinville had grown from the ashes of a past civilization; the settlement should take the name of the mythological bird that renews itself in the ashes of its own fire. The idea was accepted, and Pumpkinville was renamed Phoenix, which would become one of the largest cities in the southwest.

In the early days, Jack Swilling was one of the most prominent leaders of the Phoenix settlement. He was its first postmaster and first justice of the peace. However, once Phoenix was well established and the so-called "original town site" was located over three miles west of his holdings; he lost interest and moved his growing family back to central Arizona.

In 1878 while Swilling and two companions were on a journey into southeastern Arizona in an effort to find and bury the remains of a friend killed by Apaches, three hooded men robbed a stagecoach near Wickenburg. The description of the robbers roughly matched that of Swilling and his companions and they became suspects in the robbery. A series of legal complications brought him to Yuma where he and his companions were held in the county jail while awaiting a hearing. On August 12, 1878 Jack Swilling died in jail of natural causes before he was granted the hearing. The real robbers were identified and Jack's companions were released.

Jack was only 48 when he died, but he had lived a hard, adventure filled life. In 1931 a fountain, which stands in the park directly in front of the courthouse in Phoenix, was dedicated to

Jack and his wife Trinidad.

VIXENS, VIRUSES, AND VACCINES

I've been accused of being cynical, and often with good reason. It's been my experience that many advances in science and medicine were accomplished for an ulterior motive—generally profit.

Except for inconvenient visits to the veterinarian and the sometimes hefty vet's bills, most pet owners have never thought much about the vaccines that guard their dogs from distemper, hepatitis, leptospirosis, and rabies. However, less than a hundred years ago there were no vaccines against these common canine infections. A lot of hard work, by qualified scientists, was necessary to develop them.

When the first live, modified vaccines were produced, the last thing on anyone's mind was protection for dogs. The motivation was somewhat more commercial. The next time you see a sly old fox, tip your hat. That old villain of the local hen house played a premier role in the evolution of canine vaccines.

During the years when silver fox furs were at the height of their popularity, the Fromm brothers of Hamburg, Wisconsin, were one of the world's largest breeders. Unfortunately, silver foxes have an affinity for several deadly diseases. Because they lived in the closely bunched herds common to a fur farm, an infection, once begun, could have disastrous results. For two consecutive years, in the early 1920's a strange epidemic had been raging through the Fromm Company herds, killing the foxes before their pelts were prime and ready for harvesting. No one knew the nature of the virulent infection. The day of the lone fur trapper had only recently passed, and commercial fur farming was a relatively new enterprise. Medical knowledge concerning the diseases of previously wild animals was practically non-existent. It was obvious the fledgling fur industry was on the verge of destruction unless scientific help could be obtained to diagnose the illness and develop a suitable remedy. Many thousands of dollars were at risk.

In 1924, Dr. Robert Green, associate professor of bacteriology at the University of Minnesota offered his services to the Fromm Company. Assembling a group of expert associates, Dr. Green opened a laboratory on the fox farm. It was not until 1927, after three years of intensive study, that a virus culture was isolated from the brain and spinal cord of a dead fox. The disease produced by this virus was named, "fox encephalitis".

Early in 1930, the scope of the research had outgrown the converted warehouse on the Hamburg farm. The Fromm-Green Research Foundation, located on a bankrupt fox farm near Thiensville, Wisconsin, was established to investigate both fox encephalitis and fox distemper.

In 1936, Fromm Laboratories announced a method to give immunity to fox encephalitis by means of three injections given at three week intervals.

In May 1938, when another serious distemper epidemic broke out among the silver foxes, Fromm Laboratories was forced to attempt to halt the spread of the disease with a live, modified vaccine they had been developing, even though they were not certain it would be effective. The live, modified vaccine was a success. A major advance in disease control had been achieved.

Having developed the first effective protection against fox distemper and fox encephalitis, Fromm Laboratories began to produce their vaccines for use on other fox farms. These hard won successes opened up further possibilities in the field of animal biologics.

After laboratory and field testing of a canine distemper vaccine, Fromm announced that they could produce a vaccine which would guard dogs against distemper. As a result of the research for silver foxes, the first live modified, government approved vaccine for use in dogs was available to veterinarians everywhere.

One advance led to another. In the mid-1940's researchers discovered that infectious canine hepatitis was actually the old culprit, fox encephalitis, except the canine infection attacked the dog's liver instead of the capillary bed of the brain as in foxes. A vaccine against canine hepatitis was then developed.

One researcher noticed that there was a striking similarity between the symptoms of canine hepatitis and canine distemper, which often occur simultaneously in dogs. Research into this relationship resulted in a bivalent vaccine which gave dogs immunity against both diseases with one inoculation. Later, a single vaccine, effective against canine hepatitis, distemper, and leptospira, was developed.

Today all major biological companies produce the vaccines which were pioneered through this research.

A comparatively recent major breakthrough in animal biologics occurred in the development of a new rabies vaccine. Rabies is caused by a virus that attacks the central nervous system of the affected animal. All warm-blooded animals can spread the disease, usually by a bite which contaminates the wound with the virus in the saliva of a rabid animal. Effective vaccines were available, but they frequently had serious side effects.

Realizing the necessity for anti-rabies vaccines, but not satisfied with the danger to vaccinated pets, Fromm Laboratories conducted research into the problem. The result was an anti-rabies vaccine which contains virus attenuated in non-nervous tissue, thereby enabling your dog to be safely inoculated without the severe side effects.

Next time you take your dog to the vet for shots, remember it was the commercial value of silver fox furs that's responsible for the protection your pet enjoys today.

WORLD WALKER

Dave Kunst is the first person to be independently verified as having walked around the earth. The walk, officially credited to be 14,452 miles, took four years, three months, and sixteen days. A hardcover book, *The Man Who Walked Around the World*, published in 1979, documents the walk.

On June 20, 1970, Dave and his brother John began the epic journey from Waseca, Minnesota. The brothers carried a letter of recommendation from Sen. Hubert Humphrey, a plastic scroll, $1000 and a mule named Willie Makeit carrying camping supplies. The plastic scroll, used to document the walk, was to be stamped and signed by the mayor of every city and town where they spent the night. When Dave completed the journey he had six, five-foot long scroll sheets totally covered with the signatures of officials from around the world.

Dave and John walked to New York City where they sold the mule and flew to Lisbon, Portugal. In Lisbon they purchased another mule, named Willie Makeit II, to carry their supplies. From Portugal they walked across Spain to Monaco where they met Princess Grace.

In Venice, Italy they ran into a problem. Horses and mules were not allowed in the city because of narrow streets and pollution fears. Language was the number one problem the bothers encountered because they only spoke English. They didn't understand why the citizens of Venice were yelling and pointing at them. After the police confronted them, a major problem was resolved when the mayor finally allowed Willie Makeit II to remain in the city as long as the brothers cleaned up their pack animal's messes.

A Yugoslavian farmer gave the boys a dog which they named Drifter. When the brothers reached Turkey, Drifter was attacked and killed by Turkish sheep dogs. An American family living in Ankara, Turkey replaced the dog, which the brothers named Drifter II. The new dog didn't like walking all day so when the brothers reached Istanbul, they purchased a cart, for carrying water and supplies, and built a dog house under it so Drifter II could ride. The commander at an American Military base outside Istanbul had his men construct a canvas cover over the cart so the boys could sleep under shelter. Prior to this Dave and John had been sleeping on the open ground.

In the foothills of the Hindu Kush Mountains of Afghanistan Dave and John were attacked by bandits who believed they were carrying money in the cart. When the bandits opened fire John was killed instantly. Although Dave was wounded in the chest, he survived by pretending to be dead.

It took Dave four months to recover sufficiently from his wound to continue his journey. When he was on his feet again, Dave was joined by his other brother, Pete. Early in 1973, with the help of the American Embassy, Dave and Pete started at the exact spot in Afghanistan where John had been killed and the walk continued into Pakistan.

Dave and Pete were forced to make a detour when they were denied access to the USSR. They decided to walk to Calcutta, India where they crossed the Indian Ocean to Perth, Australia, leaving Willie Makeit III in India. With an Aussie mule named Willie Makeit IV, the brothers continued their trek. About halfway across Australia, Pete, who had taken John's place, had to return to his job in California, leaving Dave to carry on alone.

A few days after Pete left, Willie Makeit IV died of an apparent heart attack. Dave was unable to find another mule and was prepared to abandon his cart when a youngAustralian school teacher named Jenni Samuel came to his rescue. Jenni agreed to pull the cart with her car. The school teacher and the hiker proceeded a thousand miles to Sidney, Australia, with Jenni driving in second gear and Dave walking alongside the car.

Traveling such a long, slow distance together Jenni and Dave had the opportunity to get really well acquainted. They fell in love and Dave promised to return for her when he finished his walk. Dave kissed Jenni goodbye and flew from Sidney to Los Angeles, California where he resumed his epic trek.

On October 5, 1974, four years, three months, and sixteen days after leaving, David Kunst walked into Waseca, Minnesota in triumph as the first person to have walked round the earth.

As soon as possible Dave returned to Western Australia to get Jenni and bring her to the States. They married and today are living happily in Orange County, California.

During his epic walk Dave estimated he had worn out twenty-one pairs of shoes and walked approximately twenty million steps. He proved if a human being makes up his mind and is determined, he can accomplish any goal.

THE ARKANSAS MASSACRE

Some history is forgotten because we don't want to remember. Such is the case of the Elaine massacre that began on September 30, 1919 and lasted until October 7, 1919. It was by far the deadliest racial confrontation in Arkansas history and possibly the bloodiest racial conflict in the history of the United States.

Elaine is located in Philips County, part of the area known as the Arkansas Delta and borders the Mississippi River in eastern Arkansas. Phillips County had historically been developed for cotton plantations, and its land was worked by African-American slaves before the Civil War. In 1919 the county's population was still predominantly black, because most freedmen and their descendants had stayed on the land as illiterate farm workers and sharecroppers. Blacks outnumbered whites in the area around Elaine by a ten-to-one ratio, and by three-to-one in the county overall.

Although they were freedmen, most of the blacks in Philips County were kept in a form of economic slavery. All the farm land in the county was owned by whites, who thereby controlled the economy. The Negro farm workers, the sharecroppers, and the white owners were to share the profits when the crop was sold for the year. Between the time of planting and selling, the Negros were forced to buy food, clothing, and necessities at excessive prices from the store owned by the land-owner.

The landowner sold the crop whenever and however he saw fit. At the time of settlement, landowners generally never gave an itemized statement to the black sharecroppers of accounts owed, nor details of the money received for cotton and seed. The farmers were disadvantaged as most were illiterate. It was an unwritten law of the cotton country that the sharecroppers could not quit and leave a plantation until their debts were paid. The landowners made certain the debts were never paid.

Black farmers began to organize in 1919 to try to nego-tiate better conditions, including fair accounting and timely payment of monies due them by white landowners. Robert L. Hill, a black farmer from Winchester, Arkansas, had founded the Progressive Farmers and Household Union of America. Whites resisted union organizing by the farmers and often spied on or disrupted such meetings.

On September 29, approximately 100 African-American farmers met at a church in Hoop Spur, near Elaine, bringing armed guards to protect the meeting. When two deputized white men and a black trustee arrived at the church, shots were exchanged. Railroad Policeman W.D. Adkins, employed by the Missouri Pacific Railroad was killed and the other white man wounded. It was never determined who shot first.

The black trustee raced back to Helena, the county seat of Phillips County, and alerted officials. A posse was dispatched and within a few hours hundreds of white men, many of the "white trash" variety, began to comb the area for blacks they believed were launching an insurrection. Allegations surfaced that the white posse massacred defenseless black men, women and children.

Local whites requested help from Arkansas Governor Charles Hillman Brough, citing a "Negro uprising". Governor Brough contacted the War Department and requested Federal troops. After considerable delay, nearly 600 U.S. troops arrived, finding the area in chaos. Fighting in the area lasted for three days before the troops ended the violence. The federal troops disarmed both parties and arrested 285 black residents, putting them in stockades for investigation until being vouched for by their employers. There is no record of any whites being arrested.

Although official records of the time count eleven black men and five white men killed, there are estimates of from 100 to 237 African Americans killed, and more wounded. The exact number of blacks killed is unknown because of the wide rural area in which they were attacked.

In October and November 1919, an all-white Arkansas state grand jury returned indictments against 122 blacks. Since most blacks had been disenfranchised by Arkansas' 1891 Election Law and 1892 poll tax amendment, which created barriers to voter registration, blacks were non-voters, and were excluded from juries.

Those blacks willing to testify against others and to work without shares for terms as determined by their landlords, were set free. Those who refused to comply with those conditions, or were labeled as ringleaders or were judged unreliable, were indicted. According to the affidavits later supplied by the defendants, many of the prisoners had been beaten, whipped or tortured by electric shocks to extract testimony or confessions. They were threatened with death if they recanted their testimony. A total of 73 suspects were charged with murder.

The trials were held in 1920 in the county courthouse in Elaine. Mobs of armed whites milled around the courthouse. Some of the white audience in the courtroom also carried arms. The lawyers for the defense did not subpoena witnesses for the defense and did not allow their clients to testify.

Twelve of the defendants (who became known as the 'Arkansas Twelve' or 'Elaine Twelve') were convicted of murdering the white deputy at the church, and sentenced to death in the electric chair. The trials of these twelve, who were tried separately, lasted less than an hour in many cases. The juries took fewer than ten minutes to deliberate before pronouncing each man guilty. The *Arkansas Gazette* applauded the trials as the triumph of the "rule of law," because none of the defendants were lynched.

Through a series of appeals, the case of the condemned men was taken up by the U.S. Supreme Court. In *Moore v. Dempsey* (1923), the Supreme Court vacated these convictions on the grounds that the mob-dominated atmosphere of the trial and the use of testimony coerced by torture denied the defendants' due process as required by the Fourteenth Amendment to the United States Constitution.

Because the white mob actions were deemed as racial terrorism against African Americans, the deaths were classified as lynchings by the Equal Justice Initiative in its 2015 report on lynchings in the South. Based on this, Phillips County ranks as the county with the highest number of lynchings in U.S. history.

NORTON THE FIRST

There must be something in California's air that does funny things to people's minds. Over the years the golden state has produced more than its fair share of Looney Toon characters. Joshua Abraham Norton may have been the strangest of them all.

Norton was born February 4, 1818 in England, but spent most of his youth in South Africa. Upon the death of his parents he sailed west and arrived in San Francisco in November 1849. Norton initially made a small fortune as a businessman, but lost his money by investing in Peruvian rice during a Chinese rice shortage. There's no way to know for certain whether the loss of his fortune turned Joshua into one of the aforementioned Looney Toones, but that's about the time a new Joshua Norton surfaced in the historical records.

On September 17, 1859, a most unusual decree appeared in the San Francisco Bulletin newspaper. "At the peremptory request and desire of a large majority of the citizens of these United States, I, Joshua Norton, ... declare and proclaim myself Emperor of these United States; and in virtue of the authority thereby in me vested, do hereby order and direct the representatives of the different States of the Union to assemble in Musical Hall, of this city, on the 1st day of February next, then and there to make such alterations in the existing laws of the Union as may ameliorate the evils under which the country is laboring, and thereby cause confidence to exist, both at home and abroad, in our stability and integrity.— *NORTON I., Emperor* of the United States".

Although none of the representatives from any of the states convened to restructure the existing laws of the United States it didn't discourage Joshua Norton. As far as he was concerned, he was now, by proclamation, the Emperor of the United States and acted accordingly, much to the delight of the citizens of San Francisco.

During the 1860s and 70s San Francisco was perhaps the most cosmopolitan city on the west coast. For the most part the citizens enjoyed having their own crazy emperor. They looked forward to reading Emperor Norton I's zany imperial proclamations in the newspapers and thoroughly enjoyed having such a recognizable tourist attraction. Clad in an epaulette-adorned Navy coat, an ostrich feather-plumed hat and occasionally carrying a military saber, the delightfully eccentric "Emperor Norton I" walked the streets accepting mock-fealty from all who were willing to indulge his royal fantasy. He ate in restaurants free of charge, issued his own currency and made official proclamations that ranged from the comical to the surprisingly prophetic.

One of his very first royal proclamations made a great deal of sense. In October 1859, Norton declared, "fraud and corruption prevent a fair and proper expression of the public voice...in consequence of which, we do hereby abolish Congress." When Congress continued its ways of fraud and corruption, Norton ordered General Winfield Scott, commander of the United States Army, to advance on Washington and clear out the halls of Congress. Unfortunately, when Congress failed to disband and General Scott neglected to drive them from the halls of power, Emperor Norton seems to have forgotten his decree.

In 1863, when Napoleon III invaded Mexico, Joshua Norton assumed a new title, Norton I, Emperor of the United States and Protector of Mexico.

In spite of handouts the Emperor remained cash poor, so admiring subjects gave aid under the guise of paying taxes into the imperial treasury. In 1871, a local printing firm even ran off a special currency emblazoned with a picture of Norton I and his imperial seal. The Emperor passed the notes as his official government bonds until the day he died, and many recipients displayed them as treasured mementos. Today, Norton I's imperial IOUs still fetch a kingly fee among collectors.

January 8, 1880, Norton I, Emperor of the United States and Protector of Mexico, while strolling around the streets of San Francisco, dropped dead from a stroke. His death inspired headlines in dozens of newspapers, including the New York Times. The San Francisco Chronicle's headline gave Norton I a send-off fit for an Emperor. "LE ROI EST MORT" ("THE KING IS DEAD"). One paper lamented, "... no citizen of San Francisco could have been taken away who would be more generally missed." At Norton I's funeral a few days later, some 10,000 loyal subjects (some sources estimated as many as 30,000 mourners) turned up to pay their respects.

Norton had no formal political power; nevertheless, he was treated deferentially in San Francisco. Some considered him insane or eccentric, but citizens of San Francisco celebrated his imperial presence and his proclamations, such as his numerous decrees, beginning as early as 1859, calling for the city to appropriate funds for construction of a bridge and tunnel crossing San Francisco Bay to connect San Francisco with Oakland. Ignored at the time, Norton I's decree eventually came to fruition in 1936 with the opening of the Bay Bridge. There have even been campaigns to rename the bridge "The Emperor Norton Bridge".

Although Emperor Norton reigned only in obscure history, he may have been the most benevolent monarch in history. As one writer said of Joshua Norton, "since he has worn the Imperial purple [he] has shed no blood, robbed nobody, and despoiled the country of no one, which is more than can be said for his fellows in that line."

THE BRAVEST OF
THE BRAVE

Most people love military heroes who've been awarded the Medal of Honor for bravery above and beyond the call of duty. Motion pictures have been made about their exploits; such as *Sergeant York* for Alvin York, *To Hell and Back* for Audie Murphy, or the television series *Baa Baa Black Sheep* for Gregory "Pappy" Boyington. However, few people remember the man many believe was America's greatest fighting man.

Daniel Joseph Daly was born on November 11, 1873, in Glen Cove, New York. Very little is known about his life before January 10, 1899 when he enlisted in the Marine Corps, hoping to participate in the Spanish American War, which ended before he graduated from boot camp. Although Daly was a small man (5'6", 132 lbs), he quickly established himself as a Marine's Marine.

In 1900, during the Boxer Rebellion in China, Private Daly was part of a contingent of Marines tasked with defending the Foreign Legation in Peking. The Boxer Rebellion was an anti-imperialist, anti-foreign, and anti-Christian uprising that took place in China between 1899 and 1901. On August 14, Daly and Captain Hall were standing guard on the Legation wall when an extremely large group of hostile boxers approached. Captain Hall immediately went to bring up reinforcements, leaving Private Daly to defend the position single-handed. Chinese sharpshooter's filled the air with bullets as hundreds of Boxers stormed the bastion. Private Daly's steady, deadly return fire repelled repeated attacks and inflicted around 200 casualties on the attacking Boxers before reinforcements relieved him. For this gallantry Dan Daly was awarded the Medal of Honor.

In 1915, during what history calls the Banana Wars in Central America and the Caribbean, Gunnery Sergeant Daly was fighting with US forces supporting the government in Haiti against rebels. On the night of October 24, Daly was with a patrol of 40 Marines bringing supplies to Fort Dipitie when they were ambushed by a force of approximately 400 Cacos (Haitian insurgents). Gunnery Sergeant Daly immediately led his men charging directly into the ambush, disrupting and scattering the insurgents. He was awarded his second Medal of Honor for his conspicuous gallantry.

However, many old timers remember First Sergeant Dan Daily from his World War I exploits, which were widely reported in press dispatches from the front. After all, correspondents were apt to keep an eye on the only two time Medal of Honor winner deployed with the American troops in France. Dan Daily was not going to disappoint.

In June 1918 American troops had arrived in France just in time to help the devastated armies of France and England repel a German offensive that threatened to overwhelm the allied forces. There was some speculation whether the Americans had the stomach for the bloody fight. That question would be answered when elements of the Sixth Marine Regiment routed German forces in the pivotal battle for Belleau Woods, a game preserve near the village of Château-Thierry. It was at this battle the Germans were so impressed by the ferocity of the Marine forces they nicknamed the enemy "teufel hunds" (devil dogs).

On June 5th, while the Sixth Marine Regiment was moving into position, First Sergeant Daly risked his life to extinguish a fire in an ammunition dump at Lucy-le-Bocage. On June 7th, prior to the actual assault on Belleau Wood, Daly's position came under a violent artillery bombardment. It was the Marine's baptism of fire and Daly knew he needed to do something to bolster the courage of his troops. Exposing himself to the exploding shrapnel, he calmly walked along the company front visiting all the gun crews, raising everyone's moral.

As soon as the actual assault began on June 10th, the Marines came under intense machine gun fire. When the Marines faltered, First Sergeant Daly jumped up in front of his men, waving them forward and yelling, "Come on, you sons of bitches, do you want to live forever?" He attacked an enemy machine-gun emplacement unassisted, capturing it using hand grenades and his automatic pistol. On the same day, ignoring the hail of bullets all around him, he carried wounded Marines to the aid station.

For his actions at Belleau Wood, he was recommended for a third Medal of Honor. However, during the processing for his medal, someone decided awarding a third Medal of Honor to the same man was unacceptable, so Daly was awarded the Navy Cross instead.

Sergeant Major Dan Daly officially retired from the Marine Corps on February 6, 1929 and lived peacefully at Glendale, Long Island, New York, where he died on April 28, 1937.

Sergeant Major Daniel Joseph Daly was acclaimed by Major General John A. Lejeune, former Commandant of the Marine Corps, as "the outstanding Marine of all time." Major General Smedley Butler called Daly "The fightinest Marine I ever knew." Well deserved high praise for the bravest of the brave. His record as a fighting man remains unequalled in the annals of Marine Corps history.

THE LEGEND OF EL DORADO

There is something about the lure of gold that gets inside a man and takes hold of his very soul. He will do things in pursuit of treasure that he would never dare for a lesser goal. One of the golden treasures that has gripped fortune hunters for over five hundred years is the lure of El Dorado.

Many believed El Dorado, synonymous with "The Golden Place", was a mythical city supposedly located somewhere in the unexplored interior of South America. Though no one is known to have actually seen El Dorado, the fanciful tales told of an unimaginably rich city, with gold paved streets, golden temples and rich mines of gold and silver along with mountains of emeralds and other precious gems.

The Legend of El Dorado first reached the world through the Spanish conquistadores, who invaded Central America under Balboa as early as 1513. As they plundered their way into South America, the Spaniards and other Europeans heard tales of the sun-worshiping Chibcha Indians (some sources call these Indians the Muisca) who lived in the 8,600 foot high plateaus near present day Bogotá, the capital of Colombia.

The tribe, it was said, venerated gold as the sun god's metal. They wore golden ornaments and for centuries had covered their buildings with sheets of the precious metal. Some Indians spoke of a holy lake, somewhere in the mountains, that was full of gold. Others told of meeting golden chieftains in a city called

Omagua.

As the tales spread, El Dorado came to be thought of as a city of gold. It was even indicated on maps although its exact location was vague. Between 1530 and 1650 or so, thousands of Europeans braved the dangerous jungles of South American seeking the treasure. Death lurked everywhere. Venomous snakes, such as the bushmaster and the Fer-de-Lance, waited to ambush the unwary traveler. The savage Jaguar was always a danger to man and beast. Those who managed to avoid these perils still had to fear the poison arrows of native tribes who savagely defended their territory against European encroachment. The mountains were nearly impassable, and every expedition was forced to turn back when they ran out of food. More than half the men were killed and all the expeditions came to grief.

Blinded by greed and the lure of gold, the fortune hunters were searching for something that simply did not exist. There never had been a Golden City. El Dorado had been erroneously translated as "The Golden Place", when in fact the translation should have been "The Gilded One". Surprisingly, El Dorado is not a city at all—but a man.

The Chibcha Indians worshipped not only the sun, but a being who lived in Lake Guatavita. Some said it was the wife of a chief who had thrown herself in the lake centuries ago, to escape a dreadful punishment, and had survived as a goddess. Indians from all around made pilgrimages to present offerings to the goddess of the lake, and at least once a year the lake became the center of an elaborate ceremony.

Tribesmen would smear their chief with sticky resin and blow gold dust over him until he glistened from head to foot—literally El Dorado, "The Gilded One". He was then conducted in a magnificent procession to a raft on the edge of Lake Guatavita. The raft was rowed to the middle of the sacred lake, where the chief would plunge into the icy water and rinse the gold off his body, while others threw priceless offerings of gold and emeralds into the lake.

Lake Guatavita is a real lake, whose location is well known, but supporting evidence for the Gilded One remained elusive until 1969 when two farm workers found an exquisite model raft made of solid gold in a small cave near Bogotá. On board the raft were eight tiny oarsmen, rowing with their backs to the regal golden figure of their chief.

Even today Lake Guatavita still refuses to yield its golden treasures. Over the years many efforts have been made to drain the lake—by the Spanish, the French, the English (including Sir Walter Raleigh), the Colombians, and finally by an American. All those efforts ended in failure. Although some gold and emeralds were found along the muddy banks, the icy depths of the lake were never plumbed. So far as is known, the offerings to El Dorado—the Gilded One—are still at the bottom of the sacred lake.

Although El Dorado is no longer believed to be a golden city, if the lure for gold has taken hold of you, the treasure in Lake Guatavita is still waiting for someone to recover it. If you are the person able to retrieve the treasure, just beware. Your efforts might be for naught. The Columbian government is unlikely to allow you to take the gold out of the country.

A TEXAS UFO

It seems a good many of us are fascinated by UFOs and aliens. In the annals of American UFO history, few incidents have inspired as much fascination—and speculation—as the one in Roswell, New Mexico. The town of Roswell has made a tourist industry out of the supposed 1947 crash of a UFO on a nearby ranch. As the story goes, the U.S. Government hauled away the crash debris and actual alien bodies, reporting there had been no UFO. The wreckage was from a weather balloon. Whatever had actually happened, the evidence of the wreckage and the dead aliens has disappeared. All we have left is speculation.

Fifty years earlier, in 1897 at Aurora, Texas, there was an incident similar to Roswell, except the Government didn't haul away the dead alien or the space craft wreckage. The alien and the wreckage is still there—maybe. Here's the story you may never have heard.

On April 19, 1897, an article in the *Dallas Morning News* described the crash of a "mystery airship," as UFOs were known in those days. Two days earlier, at around 6am on April 17th, the airship came sailing out of the sky, smashing through a windmill belonging to Judge J.S. Proctor, before finally crashing into the ground. The debris also destroyed the good judge's flower garden. Unfortunately the pilot was killed in the collision, but locals were able to drag what was described as a "petite Martian" body from the wreckage. The alien body was buried "with Christian rites" by a traveling pastor named William Russell Taybor at the nearby Aurora Cemetery.

According to reports from residents at the time, the wreckage from the airship was disposed of in an abandoned well on the Proctor property. A later owner of the property sealed the well with a concrete slab.

Over the years, the town of Aurora didn't fare well. Struck by an epidemic and crop failures and bypassed by the railroad, the original town of Aurora almost disappeared, but the cemetery remains in use with over 800 graves.

A 1973 investigation led by Bill Case, an aviation writer for the *Dallas Times Herald* and the Texas state director of the Mutual UFO Network uncovered two new witnesses about the crash. Ninety-one year old Mary Evans, who was 15 at the time, told of how her parents went to the crash site (they forbade her from going) and heard about the discovery of the alien body. Eighty-six year old Charlie Stephens, who was age 10, told how he saw the airship trailing smoke as it headed north toward Aurora. He wanted to see what happened, but his father made him finish his chores. He told how his father went to town the next day and saw wreckage from the crash.

Bill Case then investigated the Aurora Cemetery and uncovered a grave marker that appeared to show a flying saucer of some sort. He also obtained some unusual readings from his metal detector. He asked for permission to exhume the site, but the cemetery association declined permission—according to state law, a body could only be exhumed with permission of the next of kin. Obviously there was no next of kin for the alien.

In 2008, Tim Oates, the owner of the property with the sealed well where the UFO wreckage was purportedly buried, allowed investigators to unseal the well, in order to examine it for possible debris. Water was taken from the well which tested normal except for large amounts of aluminum present. No significant pieces of anything that could be construed as debris from an airship accident were found in the well. It was stated in the report that any large pieces of metal had probably been removed from the well by a past owner of the property. No wreckage of an alien or terrestrial origin was found anywhere on the property.

In addition, the Aurora Cemetery was again examined. The grave marker that had appeared to show a flying saucer of some sort could no longer be found. Speculation was that someone, during the years between the 1973 investigation and 2008, had stolen the grave stone. Although the cemetery association still did not permit exhumation, the investigators were allowed to use ground-penetrating radar. In the area near other 1890s graves an unmarked grave was located, but the grave was so badly deteriorated, the radar could not conclusively determine what type of remains lay in the grave.

All of the accounts from 1897 agree a body "not from this world" had been recovered from the wreckage of an airship (there were no earthly airships in 1897). We may never know for certain if a space ship crashed near Aurora, Texas in 1897. Perhaps someday permission will be given to exhume the suspected grave. Now that would be interesting.

I, for one, believe an alien was actually buried in the Aurora Cemetery with Christian dignity. It has been my experience there has never been a Texan who knowingly spun a tale or stretched the truth.

WHEN HANGING DIDN'T WORK

Over the years many condemned criminals have managed to survive their trip to the gallows. Each has a unique story and I've chosen five of those stories to share with you.

First we'll meet Anne Green, a 22 year old English serving girl, who was most likely seduced by her employer's grandson. At any rate, unwed Anne became pregnant and gave birth to a premature baby boy who died soon after. After trying unsuccessfully to hide the child's body Green was accused of infanticide and in 1650 was sentenced to death by hanging. Anne Green climbed the steps to the gallows where the rope was placed around her neck and the trap door was sprung. After hanging for about half an hour Anne's body was cut down, placed in a plain wooden coffin, and sold to a local doctor who gave anatomy lectures at the university. When the doctors and others assembled for the dissection and opened the coffin they noticed the corpse was breathing. After giving her hot drinks she opened her eyes. Twelve hours after the execution Anne Green was able to say a few words. After her unique rescue the court and the public saw this as the decision of a just God and Anne Green was pardoned.

Taking her coffin as a souvenir, she settled in another town. Her father thought it a good idea to charge admission for the curious public to meet the women who couldn't be hung. The money thus earned settled all her medical and legal debts. Anne later married, had three children and lived for fifteen years after her famous execution.

Next we will consider the case of Maggie Dickson, which was similar to that of Anne Green. Maggie was a married woman living in Edinburgh, Scotland. After her husband deserted her in 1723 she was forced to seek employment by moving further south to Kelso near the Scottish Border. She found work with an innkeeper in return for basic lodgings and started an affair with the Innkeeper's son which led to her becoming pregnant. Not wanting the innkeeper to discover this because it would surely lead to her dismissal she concealed her pregnancy as long as possible. The baby was born prematurely and died within a few hours of birth. She planned to dispose of the baby in the River Tweed but couldn't bring herself to do that and finally left the corpse on the riverbank. The baby was discovered that same day and traced to Maggie. In 1724 she was convicted of infanticide, and was taken to Grasssmarket for her public hanging. After the hanging she was pronounced dead and her body was bound for Musselburgh where she was to be buried. The journey was interrupted by a knocking and banging from within the wooden coffin that must have scared the driver within an inch of his life. The coffin lid was lifted to find Maggie alive and well. The law saw it as God's will and she was freed to live with the husband who had deserted her in 1723. However, under Scottish law, since she had been officially executed, her husband was a widower. So, to legitimize their union, she was required to marry him again. Maggie lived another forty years after her execution.

Our next survivor is a man, actually a boy. In 1740, 16 year old William Duell was convicted of raping and murdering a girl in the village of Tyburn, London. Duell was sentenced to death by hanging. During this time period bodies of criminals were regularly provided to medical training colleges. After the execution Duell's body was brought to Surgeons' Hall to be dissected. After he was stripped and laid on the board one of the servants noticed he was breathing. After Duell's breath became quicker and quicker the surgeon took some blood from him (bleeding was an accepted medical treatment at that time) and in two hours he was able to sit up in his chair. That evening the authorities decided to reprieve him and his sentence was commuted to transportation (transportation was essentially a life sentence where the courts sent a criminal to a penal colony, in this case, Australia).

Our next convict survived his execution, but only for a short time. In 1752, Ewan Macdonald got into an argument with Robert Parker. When Parker tried to leave, Macdonald followed him and stabbed him in the throat. Macdonald was found guilty of murder and hanged on the town moor in Newcastle, England. His body went where most of the bodies of executed criminals went at that time—to the dissection theater of a local medical school. These corpses were very valuable to the surgeons, as they were the only legal way to study anatomy. Perhaps that explains why, upon entering the theater and finding a dazed Macdonald sitting up on the operating table, the dissecting surgeon grabbed a mallet, struck Macdonald's head, and finished the hangman's job. Many believe divine retribution was delivered years later, when the same surgeon died from a kick in the head by his own horse.

Joseph Samuel was born in England and later transported to Australia after committing a robbery in 1801. Samuel then became involved in a gang in Sydney and robbed the home of a wealthy woman. A policeman who had been sent to protect her home was murdered. The gang was soon caught and at the trial Joseph Samuel confessed to stealing the goods but denied being part of the murder. The leader of the gang was released due to lack of evidence, but Joseph Samuel was sentenced to death by hanging. In 1803, Samuel and another criminal were driven in a cart to Parramatta where hundreds of people came to watch the hanging. After praying, the cart on which the condemned were standing drove off, but instead of being hanged, the rope around Samuel's neck snapped! The executioner tried again. This time, the rope slipped and Samuel's legs touched the ground. With the crowd in an uproar, the executioner tried for the third time and the rope snapped again. This time, an officer galloped off to tell the Governor what had happened. The Governor and others believed it was a sign from God that Samuel should not be hanged, so his sentence was commuted to life imprisonment.

SUPERSTITION

Do you believe in bad luck if a black cat crosses your path? Will something dire happen if thirteen people sit down to eat at the same table? Is finding a four leaf clover a sign of good luck? Should you watch your step on Friday the 13th?

Nearly everyone has some little foible, like a good luck coin, which they believe gives them control over the mysteries of fate. Nearly everyone. However, if you scoff at all the myriad superstitions people observe, perhaps you should belong to the Eccentrics Club that meets on the 13th of each month at a London club with the sole purpose of defying popular superstitions. Umbrellas are opened indoors, salt is spilled, ladders are walked under, and waiters pour drinks into cracked or broken gasses. As far as I've been able to determine, all the members of the Eccentrics Club survive with no dire consequences. But maybe challenging superstitions isn't such a good idea.

Most British sailors have a cherished superstition that Friday is an unlucky day and Friday the 13th, particularly so. The British Admiralty decided to expose the absurdity of this notion once and for all. Sometime in the 1800s, as the story goes, the Royal Navy decided to dispel the stigma attached to Friday. They commissioned a ship and named it the *HMS Friday*. Her keel was laid on a Friday, she was launched on a Friday, and she set sail on her maiden voyage on Friday the 13th, under the command of a Captain James Friday. She was never seen or heard from again.

As you can imagine, the Admiralty has consistently and

vehemently denied the truth of this story. They claim there has never been a Royal Navy ship named *Friday*, or any other day of the week, for that matter. But the Navy's denials are unimportant because generations of British seamen have accepted every word of the story as true. It confirms their superstition and superstition cannot be overcome by logic.

In many cases superstitions survive from primitive religions when man worshiped the elements in the pious hope for help in their struggle for survival. Let's take a look at some fairly common superstitions and see where they began.

Believing that spilt salt means misfortune probably dates way, way back in time. For centuries salt was the only means of preserving meat. Since salt was not always easily obtained in primitive cultures, spilling even a small quantity could mean a shortage of preserved meat during the coming year. That doesn't explain why the antidote for spilt salt is throwing a pinch over your shoulder, but as we said earlier, logic has no place in superstitions.

For some early peoples it was essential the home be blessed with kindly spirits. The hearth was the focal point of the house where, according to the Romans, household gods lived. In western Europe the area around the fireplace was thought to be the home of the fairies who brought good luck to the household. In attempts to appease the spirits, housewives in Scotland would leave part of the fire burning in the hearth to keep the fairies warm through the night. When a family moves to a new home, it is still traditional in some parts of Britain to take the embers from the old fireplace and burn them in the new one. Even for those who don't believe in spirits or fairies, today's housewarming parties have evolved from of this old superstition.

The superstition of never allowing thirteen people to sit down to eat at the same table is generally associated with the Last Supper, when thirteen were present, including Judas Iscariot, Christ's betrayer. However, the belief is actually older than Christianity. In Norse mythology twelve gods were feasting when the spirit of strife—Loki—appeared and provoked a quarrel that ended in the death of Balder, the favorite of the gods.

One of the most widely known superstitions is the one about not walking under a ladder in case a tool or a pot of paint falls from above. One explanation is that anyone walking between the ladder and the wall is breaking the triangle—the early Christian symbol of the Trinity. Another theory is that a ladder leaning against a wall was once associated with the gallows. One method of hanging a criminal was to push the victim off a ladder so he dropped under the ladder to the rope's end.

Sometimes superstitions can bring financial rewards. Prince Urussof, a Russian nobleman, had a family superstition that the loss of a wedding ring caused the loss of the bride herself. While he and his beautiful young bride were honeymooning on the Black Sea, the wedding ring slipped off her finger and disappeared beneath the waves. The prince did the only thing he could. He bought both shores of the Black Sea from hundreds of owners for more than $40 million. He reasoned that if he owned both shores he owned the sea itself and everything that lay at its bottom. It must have worked because he didn't lose his bride. However, when the prince died his heirs no longer needed to own the ring, so they sold their property on the shores of the Black Sea for $80 million—a nice profit.

I sort of like Groucho Marx's highly individual interpretations of many popular superstitions. A black cat crossing your path signifies the animal is going somewhere. Thirteen at a table is unlucky when the hostess has only twelve pork chops. Throwing salt over the shoulder is likely to give the impression that the man who throws the salt has dandruff.

As for me, like any educated person, I don't believe in superstitions, because they aren't logical. Now if you'll excuse me, I have to search for my misplaced lucky charm.

THE POPE'S WAR
ON CATS

I have to admit cats would not top my list of favorite pets, although a fuzzy little kitten chasing a ball is about as cute as it gets. Maybe it's because cats are so doggone independent. Scientists have proven cats recognize their names, but are only going to answer to it when they feel like it. But I digress. The subject of this email is Pope Gregory IX declaring war on cats.

Now let's bear two things in mind. Pope Gregory IX didn't really declare war on cats, and I don't even know for sure that the Pope didn't like cats. After all Pope Gregory reigned during the 1230s which was a long time ago. They keep all kinds of records about Popes and their lives, but I don't think there's any mention as to a Pope's preference in pets. Actually there is a lot of evidence against the idea of a Pope, or any leader, even wanting to declare war against cats.

As you probably already know cats were brought to Europe from Egypt by the Romans and enjoyed a decent reputation for a long time—probably because they were such a boon to agricultural societies. Vermin did a number on harvests, but cats were nature's perfect solution. Cats posed no risk to the crops, but they're great at killing and eating vermin. My guess is this had something to do with ancient cat worship by people like Egyptians, who survived by farming the fertile land around the Nile.

But feline-human relations deteriorated sometime in 1233 when Pope Gregory IX issued a papal bull called *Vox in Rama*.

(A papal bull is a type of public decree, letter, or charter issued by a pope of the Catholic Church. It is named after the leaden seal (bulla) that was traditionally appended to the end in order to authenticate it.) This bull, the story goes, declared cats to be the instruments of Satan, and set Medieval Europe on a great cat purge, with special attention paid to black cats, who were particularly Satanic.

As usual a bunch of people who weren't paying all that much attention jumped to an erroneous conclusion. The most you can say about cats from this papal bull is that they are perhaps among the icons worshipped by a Satanic cult. Gregory based his edict on "evidence" from Conrad of Marburg, a papal inquisitor. Apparently torture produced some pretty convincing confessions from people who worshipped the devil and his black cat. These confessions claimed Satan was half-cat and sometimes took the form of a cat during Satanic masses.

Just digressing for a moment, you have to admit that even today black cats take a bad rap. Just think of Halloween with its black cats and witches, and the heap of bad luck you'll surely accrue when a black cat crosses your path.

However I don't think its fair to blame Pope Gregory IX for a misinterpretation. The purpose of *"Vox in Rama"* was to condemn a cult that had allegedly popped up in the Rhineland—and the bull was specifically sent to the Bishop of Mainz, Germany. So, rather than being a document banning cats from Europe, it was a letter sent to a city warning them about a cult. Your guess is as good as mine about how this papal bull became an order to exterminate cats.

Just like today's scientists come up with all sorts of wild theories about the coronavirus, yesterday's historians laid the blame for the Black Death on Pope Gregory's war against cats—without any real evidence. It isn't very likely Gregory actually condoned this massacre of cats. We know there was a massive reduction in cat populations at the time, but it's a stretch to make the connection—fewer cats, more rats, more fleas, and more plague—between Gregory and the Black Death. The abundance of rodents and the lack of their natural predators (cats) ended a hundred years <u>before</u> the plaque since the slaughter of cats stopped for the most part when Pope Gregory IX died in 1241.

First, consider the dates: Pope Gregory IX's papal bull was issued in June, 1233. The Black Death came to Europe in 1347. I suppose it's possible that *Vox in Rama* simply set the stage for a cat-killing trend that would, generations later, result in the Black Death. But this means that a papal bull that *didn't* tell people to wipe out cats and was only sent to one city somehow influenced the majority of people throughout Europe to kill off all their cats, and to stick to it over the course of the next 115 years.

If in fact the people killed off cats for over a century, it's likely there wouldn't have been many people around to be affected by the Black Death. They would have all starved because without cats to keep them under control, the vermin would have eaten all the crops.

So, in summary, Pope Gregory IX *did not* declare war on cats. Even he would have thought a kitten chasing a ball is just about the cutest thing there is.

WHEN PEPSI HAD THE SIXTH LARGEST NAVY

Have you ever bartered? You know, where rather than using money, you trade your goods or services for someone else's goods or services. That was the way people conducted commerce a couple of thousand or so years ago. However, barter can be complicated. If you had a cow to trade and wanted to obtain a horse, you had to find someone who wanted to trade a horse for a cow. Eventually people realized if they used a valuable medium to represent products they could make much less complicated trades. Hence money was invented.

There are still individuals, companies, and nations that barter deals, but they're rare because using money is generally more convenient. This is the story of a corporation bartering with a nation for enough of a military arsenal to serve an entire country in return for a supply of soft drinks.

It all began in 1959 when President Dwight Eisenhower and Soviet Premier Nikita Khrushchev decided it would be a good idea to thaw the cold war a little bit by having a cultural exchange. The U.S.S.R. began the exchange on June 10th in New York City with an exhibition of soviet technology and art. The United States reciprocated in July with the American National Exhibition in Sokolniki Park, Moscow, featuring American cars, art, fashion, an entire model American home—and Pepsi-Cola.

On July 24, then-Vice President Richard Nixon escorted Khrushchev through the American exhibition. Nixon led

Khrushchev towards a display booth that dispensed nothing other than good old Pepsi-Cola. It was a set up arranged the night before between Pepsi executive, Donald Kendall and Vice President Nixon at the American embassy. As the head of Pepsi's international division, Kendall had defied the company's leaders in deciding to sponsor a booth and attend the exhibition. To prove the trip was worthwhile, he told Nixon, he had to get a picture of Khrushchev with a Pepsi in his hand.

Nixon and Soviet leader Khrushchev got into an argument over the topic of capitalism versus communism. Their conversation got so heated Kendall intervened (was this pre-arranged?) and offered the Soviet leader a cup of his delicious, sugary beverage. A photographer caught Nixon and Khrushchev together as the Soviet leader gingerly sipped his cup of Pepsi. Khrushchev's son later recalled many Russian's first impression of Pepsi was that it smelled like shoe wax. But, he added, everyone remembered it, even after the exhibition was over.

For Kendall, the photo was a triumph. He had big plans for the brand's expansion, and the Khrushchev photo op catapulted him up the ranks at Pepsi. Six years after the American National Exhibition, Kendall became CEO.

In 1972, he succeeded in negotiating a cola monopoly with the Russians, and Pepsi syrup began flowing through the Soviet Union, where it was bottled locally. Pepsi had become a pioneer: the first capitalistic product available in the U.S.S.R. There was only one issue—money.

Soviet law prohibited taking rubles abroad and Soviet rubles were essentially worthless internationally. So the U.S.S.R. and Pepsi-Cola resorted to barter. In return for syrup, Pepsi agreed to accept an equal value of Stolichnaya vodka to distribute in the United States. The bartering worked well— Stolichnaya was popular in the United States and by the late 1980s, Russians were drinking approximately a billion servings of Pepsi a year. In 1988, Pepsi broadcast the first paid commercials on Russian TV, starring none other than Michael Jackson.

An American boycott in response to the Soviet-Afghan war

changed the entire situation between Pepsi and Russia. Russian vodka was no longer popular in America and Pepsi wanted to trade something else.

In the spring of 1989, the Russians did what any country would do in desperate times. They traded Pepsi a fleet of war ships for a whole lot of soda pop. The fleet, consisting of 17 submarines, a frigate, a cruiser, and a destroyer, was traded for three billion dollars worth of Pepsi. Wow! Three billion dollars is a lot of soda pop! Apparently Russia loved their Pepsi.

Suddenly Pepsi-Cola was the proud owner of the world's sixth largest navy—the only time in world history when a soft drink company was a world power. But it was only for a moment. The war ships were all old and outdated and had been bartered as scrap metal. Before the ink was even dry on the agreement, Pepsi sold the fleet to a Swedish company for scrap recycling.

Pepsi-Cola and Coca-Cola have been at war for years. With the sixth largest navy in the world at their disposal, Pepsi could have won that war hands down.

THE MAN WHO NEVER WAS

In late 1942, after the Allied success in the North African Campaign, military planners turned to the next target. If the Allied forces from North Africa were to attack Europe's "soft underbelly", there were two possible targets. The first option was the island of Sicily, which would open the Mediterranean Sea to Allied shipping and allow the invasion of continental Europe through Italy. The second option was to go into Greece and the Balkans, to trap the German forces between the British and American invaders and the Soviets.

The Allies preferred an invasion of Sicily, but realized the Germans suspected Sicily was the logical target and would fortify the island accordingly. What the Allies needed was some plan to dupe the Germans into thinking they were actually planning to attack elsewhere. A British officer, Lieutenant Commander Ian Fleming (who years after the war would write the James Bond 007 novels) came up with a unique plan.

Flight-Lieutenant Charles Cholmondeley and Lieutenant-Commander Ewen Montagu were given the assignment of making the plan happen. Their first task was to locate a suitable corpse, one that would pass inspection as having died in an air crash at sea. On January 28, 1943 Bentley Purchase, the coroner for the Northern District of London contacted Montagu with the news he had located a suitable body, that of a tramp who died from eating rat poison containing phosphorus. He had ingested a minimal dose not sufficient to kill him outright, but enough to impair the functioning of the liver so he died a short time later. Phosphorus is not one of the poisons readily traceable after long periods, such as arsenic.

The plan called for the body to be released at sea so as to wash up on the southwestern Spanish coast. Why Spain? While ostensibly neutral, Spain was riddled with Nazi spies. The corpse was to be the bait for a meticulous, well-connected, yet unimaginative Nazi agent active in the area - Adolf Clauss. The plan anticipated Clauss gaining access to the body and the documents it carried, but not being able to examine everything exhaustively. Spaniards, as Roman Catholics, were averse to postmortems and most likely would not hold one, especially during a war, if the cause of death obviously appeared to be drowning. Once they had a satisfactory body, Cholmondeley and Montagu painstakingly transformed the corpse into a soldier, naming him Captain (acting Major) William Martin of the Royal Marines. As a Royal Marine, Major Martin came under Admiralty authority, and it would be easy to ensure that all official inquiries and messages about his death would be routed to the Naval Intelligence Division.

They spent months creating a plausible background to make Major Martin a real person. The "wallet and pocket litter" included an identity card, ticket stubs from a movie theater, a photograph from an invented fiancée named Pam; two love letters from Pam, along with the receipt for a diamond engagement ring costing £53 10s 6d from a Bond Street jewelry shop and a message from Lloyds Bank, demanding payment of an overdraft of £79 19s 2d.. Chained to his wrist was a briefcase containing a personal letter marked "PERSONAL AND MOST SECRET", from Lieutenant General Sir Archibald Nye, vice chief of the Imperial General Staff—who had a deep knowledge of ongoing military operations—to General Sir Harold Alexander, commander of the Anglo-American 18th Army Group in Algeria and Tunisia. The letter identified Greece as the next invasion target for Allied forces. To ensure that the letters would remain legible after immersion in seawater, Lieutenant-Commander Montagu asked MI5 scientists to conduct tests on different inks to see which would last longest in the water, and then provide him with a suitable list of popular and available ink brands.

When all was in readiness, Major Martin was placed in a cylindrical canister and on April 19, 1943 loaded aboard the British submarine *Seraph*. It arrived off the coast of Huelva, Spain on April 29th. After spending the day reconnoitering the coastline, at 4:15 am on April 30th, *Seraph* surfaced. The Captain had the canister brought up on deck, then sent all his crew below except the officers. They opened the container and lowered the body into the water. The Captain read Psalm 39 and ordered the engines to full astern so the wash from the screws would push the corpse toward the shore.

When found floating near the port of Huelva, the corpse was assumed to be a British military courier who'd perished in a plane crash. The Spanish authorities agreed to a quick interment—due to the heat and stench of decomposition—and placed his belongings under lock and key.

And so the homeless Welsh tramp came to be buried with full military honors in a sunlit Spanish cemetery, under a headstone bearing the name William Martin, RM - for Royal Marines.

After a tense week or so—it took the Germans several attempts to get a look at the briefcase's contents—photographs of the falsified documents made it to Hitler's desk. He was fooled, and moved an entire panzer division—90,000 soldiers—to Greece.

And so in early July, the Allies attacked Sicily. The island fell after six weeks of fierce fighting with only a fraction of the casualties and ship losses the Allies had feared. Major William Martin had successfully completed his mission.

For those who are a stickler for details, in 1998 the British Government revealed Major Martin's true identity as Glyndwr Michael. A plaque commemorating Glyndwr Michael has been added to the war memorial in Aberbargoed, Wales. It is headed "Y Dyn Na Fu Erioed" (translation – "The Man Who Never Was").

THE AMAZING JOURNEY OF CLEMENTINE JONES

I love animal stories, but it seems most of the ones I pass along concern dogs. I don't know whether there are more cat lovers or dog lovers in the world today, but I do believe it's only fair to tell this story about one of our feline friends—Clementine Jones.

Clementine Jones, who lived with Mr. and Mrs. Lundmark in Buffalo, New York, had been named after a once popular nightclub entertainer. In 1949, Robert Lundmark was offered a position in a Denver, Colorado department store which was an upgrade both professionally and financially. The timing for the career move was not ideal since their beloved cat, Clementine Jones, was in a family way.

Mr. and Mrs. Lundmark pondered whether a pregnant cat could be moved so far without the trip being detrimental to the health of herself or her unborn kittens. They finally decided that while they did love their cat, it would be in her own best interests if she were left behind. Arrangements were made for Clementine Jones to take up residence with relatives near Buffalo in the town of Dunkirk where she could live happily and raise her kittens.

Although the Lundmarks did what they thought best, Clementine Jones had a different idea. When the kittens in her litter neared a year old and were well on their way to taking care of themselves, Clementine hit the road. Somewhere in this vast, wide land was her human family, and she was determined to find them.

She had never been out of New York State, let alone as far away as Denver, Colorado. I will never understand how the cat even knew in which direction to travel. Even if she had a map and could locate Denver, how would she overcome the obstacles in her way? There was no direct route west. She would have to skirt around Lake Michigan and cross the formidable Mississippi River.

After the cat's foster family couldn't locate Clementine Jones for nearly two months, they placed a call to the Lundmarks, who were now living in Aurora, 10 miles east of Denver. They explained the cat had been missing for several weeks and they were afraid she must have been hit by a car or killed by a predator. No one even considered the possibility Clementine Jones was somewhere in the Midwest, on her way to Colorado.

On September 18, 1950, approximately four months after leaving Dunkirk, New York, Clementine Jones turned up at the Lundmark home in Aurora, Colorado. Of course many critics claimed no cat could have made the 1600 mile journey from Buffalo to Denver. The cat that had shown up at the Lundmark home had to be a stray that simply looked like Clementine Jones. After all, it was almost impossible to believe any animal, let alone a cat, could travel over 1600 miles to find someone in a place they had never been to. In fact, even today I can hardly believe it was possible.

The cat that appeared at the Lundmark home was a black cat with a couple of white spots, but black cats with a few spots of white are not exactly rare. But the doubters would soon be silenced by Clementine Jones herself, because she had a proof of identity that couldn't be denied. She had seven toes on one of her front paws. Considering the pads on her paws were nearly worn to the bone from her 1600 mile trek, the cat who had shown up in Colorado could be none other than Clementine Jones.

Since Clementine Jones' journey was unique in the annals of cat history, the story was carried coast to coast in all the major newspapers. The story was read with more than casual interest by the owners of Coast Fishery in Los Angeles. The company had found a use for the fish they hadn't been able to sell to local stores. They ground it up and canned it as cat food, distributed under the brand name Puss'n Boots. The feline market in those days was small compared to the canine, but sales of cat food saved the company from bankruptcy. Now the wonderful story about Clementine Jones' journey was a heaven sent opportunity to show what great animals cats really are. The publicity value of giving Clementine an award for her heroic feat would be immense for Puss'n Boots brand cat food.

A local sculptor was contracted to design a medal for cats —nice looking, in thick bronze, about the size of a silver dollar coin. A proof was quickly struck, showing a recumbent cat with its paws outstretched, and bearing the inscription "The Puss'n Boots Award, Honor-Merit." The back of the medal was inscribed, "for contributing to human happiness and exhibiting other admirable traits, that further elevated the cat as man's friend and loyal companion." The medal was minted, and in early November arrived in Aurora, along with a congratulatory note,

Coast Fisheries decided Clementine Jones was merely the first of what would be many awards. They had minted dozens of Puss'n Boots medals, and decided the award should stick around as a national medal of honor for felines. From among the annual feline recipients one would be selected each year as America's "Cat of the Year" and receive a year's supply of free Puss'n Boots cat food!

Over the course of the next decade, as the accounts of the award winners hit the newspapers, they irrevocably changed the image of the American cat. Sometimes heroic, sometimes amusing, and always astounding, their real life stories touched an audience that had previously been led to believe only dogs could accomplish great things.

Meanwhile, Clementine Jones lived out her life with the family she loved, unconcerned with her fame or being the very first recipient of the Puss'n Boots medal. As long as she could sun herself on the Lundmark porch, she really didn't care she had ushered in a golden age in American feline history.

THE PUSS'N BOOTS AWARD

We've all lost something precious because the Puss'n Boots Award for cats no longer exists. The award winners gave us a new appreciation and respect for our feline friends.

Who would have guessed when a dauntless cat, wanting to find her family, showed up on a doorstep in Colorado 70 years ago, and a little fishery in Los Angeles decided to give her a medal, that a new age had dawned? For the next decade, exceptional cats were going to be acknowledged.

How about a volunteer seeing eye cat! When an elderly plantation dog went blind in Louisiana, a stray cat, who came to be known as Kitty Billy, suddenly appeared on the property. When Kitty Billy somehow sensed the dog's plight he ceased his own wanderings and began attending the blind dog. When the dog would emerge from the house, Billy would walk with it and act as its eyes, helping it safely cross streets, and making sure it eventually found its way home. Just as remarkable as what he did for the old blind dog was what he did when the old dog passed away. Billy left the plantation and never returned. He had halted his own wanderings in order to care for an ailing creature. His mission now completed, he left his medal behind to continue with his own life's journey. A selfless hero if ever there was one!

From Joplin, Missouri, came the story of a cat who adopted a litter of baby opossums. They were only a few days old when they were discovered by a Humane Society worker in the pouch of their mother, who had been hit by a car. The five baby opossums were taken to the local animal shelter where there happened to be a cat that had recently nursed her own litter of kittens. Mother Sue, as she would come to be called, stepped in to save the opossums, keeping them warm, suckling them, raising and protecting them as her own. Her medal arrived during Be Kind to Animals Week, since she was judged a symbol of the harmony that can exist within the natural world.

Another heroic momma cat was found in Reseda, California. A local stray had her litter of newborn kittens stolen by a gang of boys. When she was discovered by the Dubers family she had a swollen belly and was in extreme pain. She had been generating milk, but without her newborns to suckle she was unable to discharge it. They took her home and called a local vet. It was possible to perform an emergency operation and release the fluid they were told, but it turned out to be unnecessary. Their own family cat, Susie, had a litter of four, and picked up two by the scruff of the neck and carried them over to her ailing counterpart and coaxed them to nurse. Susie had not only correctly surmised the situation, she had offered her own kittens to aid a cat in need. The mother cat that had been deprived of her own kittens was allowed to stay in the home and keep the pair as her own.

Other cats received medals for their direct service to humankind. A Hagerstown, Maryland cat named Sandy became a hero after waking her family and saving them from a house fire. And up at San Quentin penitentiary a kitten named Chickie was the darling of the inmates. The prisoners had constructed a toy piano, a mini bed and dinner table, and a toy hot rod which Chickie rode around the prison yard. A letter of congratulation was sent by Coast Fishery, care of the prison warden, thanking Chickie for brightening the lives of 2000 men. The presentation of her medal was a cause for celebration shared equally among the prisoners and staff.

We will never know how many Puss'n Boots Awards were

presented during the relatively short life span of the award because any records that had existed, have since vanished. However, the publicity surrounding the Puss'n Boots medal winners bolstered the status of the American feline. In the process, humble neighborhood cats were being elevated to celebrity status.

Of course, it was not the kind of celebrity we're familiar with now. There was no internet to spread their fame, no YouTube to entertain millions with their antics. Compared to modern celebrity cats, the fame of the Puss'n Boots winners might therefore seem paltry. But the 1950s was a different era. Every city and even most small towns had their own newspapers, religiously read by residents, and it was there that these cats were heralded. A Puss'n Boots winner was a big deal! It was a source of pride for the entire readership, the kind of celebrity that existed on a local level. While people a few counties away may not have heard a word about it, you can bet your bottom dollar a local recipient of the Puss'n Boots Award was a bigger star than any Instagram cat could ever be.

Sadly for America's cats, and America's cat lovers, the Puss'n Boots medal had a short lifespan. This was an era that saw the growth of mega-corporations, as conglomerates bought out smaller companies and assimilated their brands. The Coast Fishery fell prey to bigger fish. Puss'n Boots cat food continued to be sold through the 1950s, and the medals likewise continued to be awarded, but they were presented with less frequency as the decade passed. The larger companies that took over the brand might be in favor of selling cat food, but were skeptical of spending the time, money, and effort to award America's finest felines with bronze medals.

The small town newspapers that heralded the fame of these cats likewise fell prey to bigger enterprises. By the 1960s they were being bought out and assimilated by larger newspapers, and these in turn were purchased by news conglomerates that owned scores of big cities papers. For news corporations there was little interest in local editions with low circulation numbers, so many small town papers were discontinued entirely.

This consolidation occurred before the digital age, so only a small fraction of the assimilated or discontinued newspapers were ever scanned and uploaded to the internet. Consequently you're not likely to find much information about Puss'n Boots winners on the Internet. Most of the information I have was from an online article by Dr. Paul Koudounaris, an historian, author, and photographer.

Times change and lifestyles evolve. However I can't help but believe we've lost something precious when we no longer honor a stray cat who volunteered to be the eyes for a blind dog.

WHO DO WE THANK FOR CHAMPAGNE?

When you think of expensive wine, chances are you'll think of French wine. And the king of champagne is, of course, French. After all the bubbly was invented (discovered?) by Dom Pierre Perignon at the abbey of Hautvilliers in 1697. But was it? No matter how vehemently the French argue the point, that ain't the way it happened.

Actually it was an Englishman, Christopher Merrett—a scientist, physician, naturalist and metallurgist—who in 1662 first documented how to put the fizz into sparkling wine. Thirty years before a monk in France's Champagne region came up with the idea, Merrett presented a paper to the newly formed Royal Society, describing how English winemakers had been adding sugar to wines to give them a refreshing, bubbly quality. It was the first time anyone had described the process or used the word "sparkling" to describe the end product. What he was actually describing was the result of secondary fermentation. Do you think it's possible Dom Perignon, a monk, would have snitched Merrett's idea?

The process of creating sparkling wine (or bubbly if you prefer) starts with fermenting the grape juice in a vat to make a conventional wine. To turn a still wine into a sparkling wine the base wine is poured into a champagne bottle with some priming sugar and yeast, a cap is put on the bottle, and the wine is allowed to ferment inside the bottle. This means the carbon dioxide can't escape, so it's retained in the wine in the bottle and that gives us the bubbles when the top is popped off.

For French winemakers, secondary fermentation was a menace. The build-up of gas caused their rather flimsy glass bottles to explode, and when one went bang it could set off its neighbors as well, devastating entire cellars. (Just a short aside. Wine bottles can explode if the fermentation process for still wine isn't completed before bottling. My brother made his own wine, and lost a batch when he bottled it too soon. When we summoned the courage to check out the basement, hoping to avoid any more exploding bottles, we found an unbelievable mess.)

But for English winemakers, secondary fermentation and the magic it added was a boon, not a burden. Their wine bottles were heavier and thicker—like modern champagne bottles —much less likely to explode.

Apparently the Royal Navy is to thank for the thicker bottles. Early modern glassmakers used charcoal made from oak to heat their furnaces. However, oak was required to build the ships England needed to patrol the seas. The British Admiralty banned the use of oak for anything other than shipbuilding. English glassmakers, forced to seek out other fuels, turned to coal and discovered it burned hotter and allowed them to make stronger glass.

Okay, if champagne was invented (discovered?) by the English, why is it called champagne after the region in France where Dom Perignon first made his bubbly wine? I don't want to hurt anyone's feelings, but the French, hands down, had the superior public relations department. Everything is in the name.

All sparkling wine is made exactly the same way, with secondary fermentation in the bottle. Unless you're one of those fancy wine types, you may not know that there's no such thing as British champagne. Champagne is sparkling wine produced in, you guessed it, Champagne, France.

Although Christopher Merrett first documented how to put the fizz in sparkly wine in 1662, the British produced very little sparkling wine over the next two hundred plus years. The art of making sparkling wine had a resurgence in the early twentieth century. So the question was, what's sparkling wine made in Britain, with British grapes, to be called? Well, before this, nothing. It was just called 'sparkling wine made with English, Scottish, or Welsh grapes'.

You can see where this would be a promotional problem. Here is a couple celebrating their fiftieth wedding anniversary by popping the cork on a bottle of Champagne. Or here is the same couple popping the cork on a bottle of sparkling wine made with English, Scottish, or Welsh grapes. Somehow that doesn't resonate with the same romantic connotations.

It's not like the British haven't been trying to come up with a name to compete with Champagne. Actually a New York bar owner, Jason Hicks, started using 'British Fizz' on his wine lists. Bob and Sam Lindo, of the UK Vineyard Association, saw the menu, liked the name, and are now in the process of applying for protected geographical indication for the term, which will mean that only sparkling wines made with grapes grown in England, Wales, or Scotland will be able to use the name.

I'm not the person you should turn to for name approval but I don't think British Fizz will become a household name. To me it sounds like a soda pop and brings to mind images of carbonated water. Perhaps they should call it Winchcombe in honour (note the English spelling of honor) of the picturesque Cotswold town of Winchcombe where Christopher Merrett first documented "how to put the fizz into sparkling wine". Then again maybe they should just stick with English Sparkling Wine. I certainly like that name better than British Fizz.

AN AMAZING ESCAPE

Serving aboard a submarine is a very chancy occupation. When a submarine sinks, most likely the entire crew will perish. Of all the submarines and crews lost during WW II, there are only four documented cases of men surviving a submarine sinking. This is the story of one of those men.

When she left the British submarine base at Malta at the end of November 1941, *HMS Perseus* had on board 59 crew members and two passengers. One of those passengers was John Capes, a 31 year old British Navy stoker hitching a ride to the British submarine base at Alexandria, Egypt.

Toward the end of 1941, the Mediterranean was pretty much a German lake. In order to operate in the area, British submarines traveled submerged during the day, coming to the surface only at night to charge their batteries. Thus, on the rough winter night of December 6th, *Perseus* was on the surface two miles off the coast of Kefalonia, recharging her batteries under cover of darkness in preparation for another day underwater.

Since John Capes was a passenger and not a working member of the crew, he had been able to smuggle a bottle of rum aboard. Being a bit tipsy may have been partially responsible for his survival. Capes was relaxing in a makeshift bunk, converted from a spare torpedo tube, sipping from his bottle of rum when, with no warning, there was a devastating explosion. The boat twisted, plunged, and hit the bottom with what Capes described as a "nerve-shattering jolt". His bunk reared up and threw him across the compartment. The lights went out.

Capes guessed the submarine had hit a mine. He groped in

the pitch blackness until he found an emergency lantern. In the increasingly foul air and rising water of the engine room he found "the mangled bodies of a dozen dead". The engine room door was forced shut by the pressure of water on the other side. "It was creaking under the great pressure. Jets and trickles from the rubber joint were seeping through," said Capes.

He continued searching until he found three injured men, dragging them towards the escape hatch. He then located the Davis Submerged Escape Apparatus sets which are life vests with a rubber lung, an oxygen bottle, mouthpiece and goggles, and handed them to the men. The plan was to exit the doomed submarine via the escape hatch and breathe with the Davis Submerged Escape Apparatus until they reached the surface. This equipment had only been tested to a depth of 100ft, and the depth gauge next to the escape hatch showed a depth of just over 270ft. As far as Capes knew, no one had ever made an escape from such a depth where the water pressure was enough to crush a man. Death was certain if he remained in the sub, so he decided he might as well take his chances with the water pressure. Unknown to Capes the depth gauge was broken, and the sub was actually lying at a depth of a 170ft.—which was still 70ft beyond the tested limits of the Escape Apparatus.

It was getting difficult to breathe in the thick, foul air as he struggled to release the damaged bolts on the escape hatch. He gave his injured companions a drink of his rum for liquid courage as he pushed them up through the hatch and away into the cold sea above. Then he took a last swig of rum from his blitz bottle, ducked under and passed through the hatch himself.

"I let go, and the buoyant oxygen lifted me quickly upward. The pain became frantic, my lungs and whole body as fit to burst apart. Agony made me dizzy. How long can I last? Then, with the suddenness of certainty, I burst to the surface and wallowed in a slight swell with whitecaps here and there."

His fellow injured stokers had not made it to the surface with him so he found himself alone in the middle of a cold December sea. He had no idea where he was, but spotted a band of white cliffs and realized he had no choice but to swim in that direction. Having made the deepest escape yet recorded, his ordeal was not over.

The next morning, Capes was found unconscious by two fishermen on the shore of Kefalonia. For the next 18 months he was passed from house to house by friendly islanders, to evade the Italian occupiers. He was finally taken off the island on a fishing boat in May 1943, in a clandestine operation organized by the Royal Navy. A dangerous, roundabout journey of 640km took him to Turkey and from there back to the submarine service in Alexandria.

Despite being awarded a medal for his escape, Capes' story was so extraordinary that many people, both within and outside the Navy, doubted it. Had he actually been on the boat at all? After all, he was not on the crew list. And submarine commanders had been ordered to bolt escape hatches shut from the outside to prevent them from lifting during depth charge attacks. There were no witnesses, and his written accounts after the war varied in their details. The depth gauge reading of 270ft made his story all the harder to believe.

John Capes died in 1985 with his amazing story of escape still in doubt by many. Then in 1997 the wreck of *Perseus* was found in 170 feet of water, two miles off the coast of Kefalonia where Capes had said it would be. In a series of dives to the wreck Kostas Thoctarides discovered Capes's empty torpedo tube bunk, the hatch and compartment exactly as he had described it, and finally, his blitz bottle from which he had taken that last fortifying swig of rum. Thoctarides also saw the broken depth gauge which still read 270 feet. At last John Capes' story was verified, and as far as I know, he still holds the record for the deepest escape in history.

The atomic submarines of our modern Navy are much safer and more reliable than the old diesel subs of John Capes' day. However, submarine duty is still hazardous for the men and women who serve. Personally, I prefer dry land under my feet.

AMAZING
COINCIDENCES

Of the four Presidents who have been assassinated while in office—Abraham Lincoln (1865), James A. Garfield (1881), William McKinley (1901), and John F. Kennedy (1963)—two in particular have captured the attention of the American public.

It was quickly determined the assassins of Garfield and McKinley were obviously mentally deranged. Consequently there have been no great conspiracies, real or imagined, concerning those assassinations.

That is not the case with Lincoln or Kennedy.

Because JFK was a more contemporary figure most of us are aware of the numerous books written about all sorts of conspiracy theories. How about the mysterious second shooter supposedly on the grassy knoll in Dealey Plaza? Or did organized crime figures orchestrate the assassination? Even an exhaustive government investigation via the Warren Commission, did nothing to dispel the conspiracy theories.

I can assure you there were just as many, if not more, books written about the theories surrounding Lincoln's assassination. Was a member of Lincoln's own cabinet behind the planning of the crime? Did Mrs. Lincoln, who was born in the South, have something to do with the murder of her husband? The theories go on without end.

Perhaps because people get so wrapped up in their favorite conspiracy theory, they dream up all sorts of cosmic karma linking JFK and Lincoln. However, in obscure history the lives and the assassinations of Lincoln and Kennedy are actually linked by an amazing series of coincidences. Here is a list of those coincidences gathered by historians (?) with way too much time on their hands.

Abraham Lincoln was first elected to Congress in 1846. John Kennedy was elected to the Senate in 1946.

Lincoln was elected as the 16th President of the United States on November 6, 1860. Kennedy was elected to be the Republic's 35th President on November 8, 1960.

Both lost a son while living in the White House. Lincoln's 11-year-old son, William, died from typhoid fever. Kennedy's infant son, Patrick died from infant respiratory distress syndrome.

John Wilkes Booth, the man who killed Lincoln, was a Southern sympathizer born in 1838, while Lee Harvey Oswald, Kennedy's killer was Southern born in 1939. Both were themselves shot and killed before they could be brought to trial.

John Wilkes Booth and Lee Harvey Oswald both have 15 letters in their names. (Whoever took the time to count the letters of each name really needs to get a life.)

Booth shot Lincoln in Ford's Theatre, and was caught in a barn (warehouse) in Virginia. Oswald shot Kennedy from the Texas School Book Depository, which was a warehouse, and was arrested in a movie theater.

Both Lincoln and Kennedy had forebodings of their impeding deaths.

On the day he was assassinated, Lincoln told a guard, William H. Cook, "I believe there are men who want to take my life, and I have no doubt they will do it. If it is to be done it is impossible to prevent it."

On November 22, 1963, Kennedy told his wife, Jackie, and his personal adviser Ken O'Donnell, "If somebody wants to shoot me from a window with a rifle, nobody can stop it, so why worry about it?" Kennedy was shot a few hours after making this statement.

Lincoln and Kennedy were both historic civil rights cam-
paigners. Kennedy was concerned with racial equality and was
the first to propose what would become the Civil Rights Act of
1964. Lincoln felt strongly that all slaves should be freed and
issued the Emancipation Proclamation, which was the first step
in legally freeing all slaves. (The Emancipation Proclamation
actually only freed the slaves in States in rebellion against the
United States. All slaves were freed by the 13th Amendment
ratified in 1865.)

Both were shot in the back of the head on a Friday while
their wives were sitting beside them.

Lincoln was shot in Ford's Theater. Kennedy was shot in an
automobile made by the Ford Motor Company—a Lincoln.

One final, unhappy coincidence is Kennedy had a secretary
named Lincoln—Evelyn Lincoln—who reportedly advised him
against going to Dallas.

All these coincidences are true, but the list is probably
more fun than significant. I doubt whether Kennedy's assassination was an example of history repeating itself. But who
knows? Maybe there is something to all this.

PROHIBITION AND PRESCRIPTIONS

Chances are that Prohibition came and went before you were born, but some businesses that thrived because of prohibition are still around. It would not be a stretch to say the growth in their popularity can be directly traced to prohibition.

The Eighteenth Amendment of the U.S. Constitution, ratified on January 16, 1919 prohibited the manufacture, sale, or transportation of intoxicating liquors in the United States, though it did not outlaw the actual consumption of alcohol. Shortly after, Congress passed the Volstead Act to provide for the federal enforcement of Prohibition.

The Volstead Act – otherwise known as the National Prohibition Act – had a few loopholes. Not only was sacramental wine an exception to the rule, but also "medicinal" booze. "Medicinal" booze was a really big loophole. Prescription booze could be used to treat a laundry list of ailments, including sore throats, toothaches, the flu, and more. A prescription from a doctor permitted those suffering from mild ailments to legally purchase a pint of alcohol for "pharmaceutical" reasons. And where could you find this so-called medicinal liquor? At a drug store, of course. Every 10 days, prescription in hand, patients who wanted to buy alcohol could do so quite easily at legit pharmacy chains. I never found out whether the Doctor's prescription could specify Scotch, Brandy, Bourbon, etc., as the preferred medicine.

Partly because of this, drug stores flourished, and Walgreens, in particular, grew exponentially. The chain expanded from around 20 stores in 1919 to more than 500 stores by the early 1930s. Walgreens began in 1901, with a small food front store on the corner of Bowen and Cottage Grove Avenues in Chicago, owned by Galesburg, Illinois native Charles R. Walgreen. However, Walgreens phenomenal growth wasn't due solely to prescription alcohol.

Do you remember the soda fountains that existed in many drug stores? History doesn't record who invented soda fountains. I suspect it was some overworked clerk who never gained any recognition for the idea which caught on all over the country. By the early 1920's just about every drugstore had a soda fountain. Many historians believe the reason for the explosion of soda fountains was most likely that prohibition began in 1919 and the soda fountain filled the social void caused by the closing of bars. Although soda fountains are difficult to find today (they might not even exist anymore), I fondly remember them from my youth. In addition to ice cream treats, soda fountains also frequently served sandwiches and functioned as lunch counters for shoppers and downtown workers.

Some of Walgreens phenomenal growth could be credited to the prohibition driven soda fountain, but also the 1922 invention of the malted milkshake. Again history doesn't record the name of the individual who invented the malted milkshake (or even the milkshake itself), although it is generally acknowledged the soda fountain treat was first served in a Walgreens drug store. Back in the 1920s customers stood three and four deep around the soda fountain to buy the "double-rich chocolate malted milkshakes." My mouth still waters at the memory of all the vanilla, chocolate, or strawberry malted milkshakes I consumed at soda fountains.

Historical purists will quickly point out, and rightfully so, that malted milk was first invented by William Horlick of Racine, Wisconsin, perhaps as early as 1870. A patent was filed in

1883, and it was introduced to the market in 1887. It was a mixture of powdered whole milk, malted barley, and wheat. Malted milk was marketed as a health food in powder or pill form. I believe Horlick Malted Milk is still sold in stores (so you can make your own malted milkshakes).

Just to keep the record straight, Walgreens was the first to mix the malted milk powder with ice cream to create the malted milkshake. Although many locations still sell malted milkshakes, they haven't been called that for many years. Recently I pulled into a drive through at a fast food franchise and ordered a vanilla malted milk. The order taker apologized that they didn't carry malted milk. I was going to protest because it was plainly printed on the menu but it dawned on me I was dealing with a new generation. I changed my request to a vanilla malted and the young lady had no problem filling my order.

At any rate, with the help from prescription booze and the malted milkshake, Walgreens continued to grow and expand. Today, the chain has more than 9,200 locations in the U. S., which is second only to CVS's 9,900 locations. And neither chain fills "medicinal" booze prescriptions or has a soda fountain.

I personally think the loss of soda fountains is an unfortunate victim of history. Even writing about it makes my heart smile when I remember sitting at a soda fountain, sharing a chocolate malted (two straws, one malt) with my grade school sweetheart.

THE WORST SUBWAY DISASTER

Most New Yorkers, even station agents and train conductors on the New York subway system, have never heard of the Malbone Street wreck, so it's no surprise if you've never heard of the worst mass-transit accident in New York City history.

On November 1, 1918, the Brotherhood of Locomotive Engineers went on strike. The Brooklyn Rapid Transit System (BRT) was determined to keep the subway system running during the strike, so they used scabs. (A strikebreaker—sometimes derogatorily called a scab—is a person who works despite an ongoing strike. Strikebreakers are usually individuals who were not employed by the company prior to the trade union dispute, but rather hired after or during the strike to keep the organization running.).

With hardly any training, 23-year-old Brooklyn Rapid Transit employee Edward Luciano became a scab motorman. Many people think because a subway car runs on tracks a motorman has very little to do except stop and start the train. Actually, especially in 1918, quite a bit of training was required to safely operate the complex braking maneuvers necessary to ease the wooden five-car train along the curving tracks. In addition to little training, Luciano had already been on the job for 10 consecutive hours, when he was assigned to drive a rush-hour Brighton Beach Line train (today's B and Q line) from Manhattan to the edge of Brooklyn.

The strike had caused delays, so the train was behind schedule when Luciano took over. He was unfamiliar with the challenging route, and although he was already exhausted, he was being pressured to make up lost time. It would be difficult to envision a scenario more likely to lead to disaster.

It was obvious early on that Luciano was having difficulty. His driving was so erratic passengers exited in droves at the preceding stations, emptying the train by half. Still, more than 400 passengers were inside when tragedy struck.

Luciano took a hairpin S-curve in a 6-mph zone at 44 mph. The train jumped the track and crashed into a concrete wall. The wooden car roofs were sheared off. Glass from broken windows impaled bodies. The crash was heard a mile away and the screams of the victims carried to the street, where a ticket seller called for the police. Rescue attempts were hindered by the jam of debris in the narrow tunnel. Apparently the first car crashed into the tunnel wall and the other cars smashed into it, grinding the car to splinters and crushing the people inside. BRT electricians, not knowing the third rail had been ripped up in the wreck, restored power electrocuting dozens of survivors limping to safety.

Edward Luciano, the motorman, physically unscathed, ran home in hysterics.

The 1918 Spanish Flu pandemic had filled all the hospital beds so those injured in the crash were taken to Ebbets Field (home of the Brooklyn Dodgers baseball team) which became a makeshift hospital. In all, the reported death toll ranged from 93 to 102, with approximately 250 injuries.

A historic and sensational lawsuit was brought against the BRT following the accident, marking "the first time railroad management was brought to account for a fatal accident". The BRT went bankrupt the very next month and eventually returned as the BMT, or Brooklyn-Manhattan Transit Corp.

From even the most horrendous tragedy often comes some good. Those who died that day live on in the safety measures their deaths inspired. In response to the cry for improved safety measures, "trippers," a concept still in use today, were implemented to prevent trains from speeding and running red signals. The "dead man's switch" was also birthed in the aftermath of the wreck: Should a motorman die, or let go of the controls for some other reason, a dead man's switch will bring the train to a halt.

While the waves of change in the wake of the catastrophe are difficult to measure so many years later, it's easy to count the physical reminders, because there are so few. Even Malbone Street was rechristened Empire Boulevard, because the old name was too full of death.

And what of Edward Luciano who had been driving the train that fateful afternoon? After investigations and trials Luciano was found innocent of any wrong doing. But the legacy of the wreck haunted him. He changed his name to Anthony Lewis and became a house builder in Queens Village, Queens. He retired in Tucson, Arizona, where he died in 1985 at the age of 91.

In November 2019, officials installed a permanent bronze memorial plaque at the northern exit of the Prospect Park station, and co-named the corner of Empire Boulevard and Flatbush Avenue as "Malbone Centennial Way". The plaque inscription reads:

Remembering the Malbone Street Wreck
In memory of those who lost their lives near this location on November 1, 1918, when a wooden-bodied train carrying an estimated 650 passengers derailed and crashed under Malbone Street. Nearly 100 people were killed, and nearby Ebbets Field was turned into a makeshift hospital to care for the hundreds injured. This horrific accident led to meaningful reforms and advancements in transit safety, training and infrastructure. As a result of this tragedy, Malbone Street was eventually renamed and is today known as Empire Boulevard.

* * *

1918 was an unprecedented year of death all around the

world. World War I which had claimed millions of lives ended November 11, 1918, and the Spanish Flu was in the process of killing people by the millions. Perhaps that's why the 100 or so deaths in this accident were quickly forgotten by all but their loved ones.

THE FLYING FEMINIST

If I asked you to name the top female aviation pioneers, most people would immediately name Amelia Earhart. Even those who could name some other early female aviators, would not likely come up with the name Lilian Bland. Yet, at one time the world knew Lilian as The Flying Feminist. Pioneering aviator Lilian Bland had built and flown her own plane before Amelia Earhart had even become a teenager. So why don't more people know her name?

Born on September 28, 1878, into a wealthy family at Willington House in Kent, England, Lilian had never had any interest in the empty lives, full of empty talk, of the society ladies of the Edwardian era. She was imaginative and artistic and loved to flaunt conventions. At a time when ladies simply did not break the rules, she smoked cigarettes, hunted hare and fox, fished, practiced jujitsu, fired guns, and watched car races. She preferred pants over skirts and riding astride to sidesaddle. Once a priest in Tipperary actually urged spectators to stone her because of the way she rode on a horse.

On July 25, 1909, Louis Blériot, a Frenchman, became the first person to fly a heavier than air craft across the English Channel—a flight that took 36 minutes and 30 seconds, before crashing in an English field. Postcards celebrating his achievement were quickly printed and sold. Lilian Bland's uncle sent her one of those postcards and Lilian was immediately bitten by the flying bug.

She attended the first official British aviation meeting at Blackpool in October 1909 and studied the aircraft on display, scribbling down their dimensions and measurements. To anyone who would listen, she announced plans to make a plane that would fly and was met with scorn. "Hoots and derision—which did not worry me at all," she later wrote. It was only six years after the Wright brothers had made their first flight in North Carolina in 1903, and Amelia Earhart was then only 12 years old.

With the sketch of the biplane she was planning to build firmly in hand, Lilian returned home to Tobercooran House in Carnmoney, a town north of Belfast, Ireland, where her father, John Humphrey Bland, had moved after the death of his wife, Lilian's mother.

Lilian approached the task of building a flying machine in a methodical manner. First she built a biplane glider with a six-foot wingspan to test whether her design would even fly. When the model flew quite well, Lilian began constructing a full size glider to test how much weight it would carry. The workshop where she worked was small, so Lilian finished the plane, section by section, carrying each piece to the coach house for assembly. The wingspan, when finished, was 27 feet, 7 inches

Lilian completed her glider in 1910, and christened it *Mayfly* in a deliberate nod to her critics who had joked—*it may fly, or it may not*. To test its weight-lifting capacity, she enlisted four six-foot volunteers from the Royal Irish Constabulary (police officers), along with her aunt's garden assistant, Joe Blain, to hold on to the wings as she took off. Even with all the weight, the *Mayfly* rose steadily in the wind that blew up Carnmoney Hill. The hangers-on, panicked by the quick loss of earth beneath their feet, let go within seconds of the *Mayfly's* rise, but Lilian now knew for certain if the glider could lift the weight of five men, it could handle the weight of an engine.

She ordered a light 20 horsepower two-stroke engine from A. V. Roe & Co. for £100, and after some delays brought it to Carnmoney where she installed it in the *Mayfly*.

Finally, in September of 1910, she was ready. Lilian climbed into the cockpit. Joe Blain, standing between the tail booms, began swinging the propeller with a whip of his arms. The *May-fly* took off—after a few stuttering bounces—rising to 30 feet for a quarter of a mile and scattering bystanders below. Not only did this make Lilian the first woman to fly an aircraft in Ireland, but the *Mayfly* also became the first powered biplane in Ireland. "I have flown!" Lilian wrote to Flight magazine, describing her feat. She was triumphant.

Lilian's father, who considered her aviation pursuits "dangerous and unbecoming," made her an offer: He would buy her a new Model-T Ford if she gave up flying. Lilian agreed, and within weeks the engine was sold. The Mayfly was donated as a glider to a local boys' club. "I had proved wrong the many people who had said that no woman could build an aeroplane, and that gave me great satisfaction," said Lilian.

Though Lilian would later be referred to in the Irish press as the "flying feminist" for her groundbreaking accomplishment, for the rest of her life, her interest in planes seemingly disappeared—a reason, perhaps, there is scant mention of her in history books: She was no full-blown aviator nor was she just a photographer or journalist or artist or martial artist. She was many things, at a time when women were largely expected to be just two—wife and mother.

On October 3, 1911 Lillian married her cousin Charles Loftus Bland, a lumberjack from British Columbia who had returned to Ireland to propose to Lilian. The couple emigrated to Canada where they built their own farm on virgin lands. Charles and Lilian had their first and only child, Patricia Lilian Bland, on April 13, 1913. Patricia died of tetanus in September 1929, at the age of 16. The couple separated soon after, with Lilian returning to England.

When asked in 1966 by a reporter for the Western Morning News what she thought of airplanes, 88-year-old Lilian Bland—the first woman in the world to build and fly her own plane—didn't miss a beat. "Noisy things," she said.

Lilian Bland died at the age of 92 on May 11, 1971. Somehow I suspect she didn't really care whether the history books recognized her flying accomplishment. She had done something the critics had said was impossible, and that was good enough for her.

THE ONLY SPACE CAT

During the early years of space flight the first astronauts were animals. The idea was to gauge the effects of spaceflight on living creatures in the hopes that humans could follow. It's hard to believe now after we've had humans walking on the moon, but when man first had the technology to reach for the stars there were serious concerns whether the human body could withstand the physical challenges of space flight.

On November 3, 1957, the Soviet Union launched Laika, a stray dog found on the streets of Moscow, into space on Sputnik 2. She died in space, but was the first animal to orbit the Earth. On January 31, 1961, as part of Project Mercury, the chimpanzee Ham became the first hominid launched into space for a suborbital flight. On November 29, 1961, Enos became the second chimpanzee launched into space, and third hominid after cosmonauts Yuri Gagarin and Gherman Titov, to achieve Earth orbit. France's base in the Sahara launched a rat named Hector on February 22, 1961, causing France to become the third country to launch animals into space. Hector had electrodes implanted on his skull so neurological activity could be monitored.

Most of us probably don't even think of France when we think of the pioneers of space exploration. The United States, Russia, and more recently China, have gotten all the space related headlines. However, France actually did quite a bit of experimentation during the 1960s and 70s.

After the successful experimentation with rats, French scientists wanted to use larger mammals and chose cats. The space program purchased 14 cats, all females, from a pet dealer, with the individual animals selected based on their temperament and calm demeanor. The cats were unnamed prior to the launch to reduce the likelihood the scientists would become attached to them. All of the cats had permanent electrodes surgically implanted into their brain to assess neurological activity.

I don't know about all the animals sent into space, but the French cats actually trained for their space flight. Some of the cats' training was even similar to training for humans, including using the high-G centrifuge.

The French cats trained for two months before six feline finalists were selected on October 17th as candidates for the flight. Then on launch day, October 18, 1963, a black and white cat, known as C 341, was chosen for the actual flight. Weighing in at 5.5 lbs, C 341 was selected as the best of the six finalists due to her calm demeanor and appropriate weight.

At 8:09 am, October 18th from the French launch site in Algeria, C 341 was launched into space atop a Véronique AG1 rocket. The cat's rocket sped upward at six times the speed of sound and exposed her to 9.5 g's of force. The nose cone separated from the rocket upon reaching a height of 94 miles above the Earth, where C 341 briefly experienced weightlessness. Fifteen minutes later, she safely returned to Earth by parachuting down in her little space capsule, alive and well. And just like that, an unsuspecting black and white kitty plucked from the streets of Paris became a space cat celebrity— the first cat to reach space.

The media immediately named C 341 "Félix" after the Félix the Cat cartoon series. The French Space Agency changed it to the feminine Félicette and adopted the name as official. Félicette was euthanized two months after the launch so that scientists could examine her body to observe the effects of spaceflight.

France continued its biological payload research, changing to monkeys. A monkey known as Martine was launched on March 7, 1967 and another monkey, Pierrette, was launched six days later. They were both successfully recovered. France concluded biological payload research with these flights, but worked on biological payloads with the Soviet Union in the 1970s.

Then, Félicette, the first and only feline to ever travel to space, was all but forgotten. So forgotten that in the 1990s, when three former French colonies celebrated her story by issuing postage stamps with the cat's likeness, they mistakenly turned her into a boy by using the wrong name—Felix.

The Soviet Union's first dog in space, Laika, was honored as a national hero. Ham, the American space chimpanzee, was famously buried at the International Space Hall of Fame in New Mexico, but Félicette was simply forgotten for more than half a century.

Finally a movement to honor Félicette raised $57,000 to commission a statue. On December 18, 2019, a statue was unveiled at the International Space University in Strasbourg, France. Félicette's bronze likeness stands on an Earth globe, her keen kitty eyes fixed on the skies where she once soared higher than any cat in world history.

A FORGOTTEN
WARRIOR

This is Ed's story.

I met Ed in the fall of 1957 when he asked if he could join me at my table in the slop chute (snack bar). He was an old man, all of at least thirty-five or -six (I was nineteen). During the next several months he told me his story over a few beers. I never did learn why he was still a buck sergeant (three stripes) after seventeen years in the Corps, but I suspect it was because he liked his beer a little too much. These are Ed's stories and I can't vouch for his veracity, but I never had any reason to doubt him.

Ed had been raised in an orphanage and wasn't certain about his birthday or exactly how old he was, although he figured his age was correct within a year one way or the other. In 1940, he had been living on the streets when a kindly judge gave him a choice; either join the Marine Corps or go to jail for stealing food. Ed chose the Corps and had been a Marine ever since. When he graduated from boot camp he was assigned to a defense battalion and shipped to the Pacific. The defense battalions occupied islands and fortified them in the expectation there would be a war with Japan. The best known islands the defense battalions occupied were Wake Island, Midway, and Guam. Ed never made it to any of the big islands.

He was stationed on a no name island somewhere in the Pacific. It was small, maybe a mile long and half a mile wide, with no water and no strategic value at all. He had no idea why he was stationed there with twenty Marines and a sailor. The sailor was in command of the lone rowboat on the island. Since there was no anchorage, supply ships anchored out from the island and the sailor had to row out to pick up supplies, including water, and occasionally the mail. (I never saw Ed receive a letter at mail call, probably because he didn't have anyone to write him.)

Life on the island was pretty much unrelieved boredom. I don't remember all of the things Ed and the Marines did to relieve the boredom, and some of the stuff isn't fit to report to a genteel audience. Suffice it to say that when war broke out in December 1941 and the Japs hit Wake Island, the Philippines, and Pearl Harbor, they didn't bother with Ed's island. In fact Ed figured everyone, including the Marine Corps, had forgotten his little island even existed. By this time Ed didn't care. According to him most of the guys in the defense battalions were at least a little psycho (Ed was still a bit strange when I knew him). However they were evacuated by submarine and taken to Pearl Harbor where they were reassigned to combat outfits. According to Ed most of the defense battalion guys just didn't give a damn anymore and the majority were killed in the early battles.

Ed participated in the assault at Guadalcanal (America's first offensive action of WWII) where he got malaria and dengue fever. He also fought at Saipan and Iwo Jima before rotating to the states. He was awarded the Navy Cross (second only to the Medal of Honor as an award for valor) for an action on Iwo Jima. I don't know how he earned the medal because he refused to talk about it. When I asked him, he only said, "I didn't do anything special. Every one of those damn kids should have earned at least a Navy Cross."

When the Korean War broke out in 1950, Ed participated in the amphibious landing at Inchon. From there he fought his way up the eastern side of North Korea, all the way to the Chosin Reservoir.

The Korean War is pretty much the forgotten war and most

of you probably don't remember the Chosin Reservoir, which was one of the epic battles (in my opinion) of American history.

In November, 1950, 300,000 Chinese troops crossed the Yalu River and struck the American troops in North Korea. Half of the Chinese force completely routed the 8th Army forces on the western side of Korea. Three days after Thanksgiving 150,000 Chinese hit the 8,000 Marines at the Chosin Reservoir. Against human waves of communist troops, the Marines cut them down by the hundreds and managed to hold their ground. However, the Chinese surrounded the Marines. In sub zero temperatures and overcast skies (so there was no air support) the Marines made their stand.

Trapped on a hill near the village of Yudam-ni, Ed remembered mostly the bitter cold. Rifles and machine guns froze and the men had to urinate on them before they would thaw enough to fire. They could see thousands of enemy troops swarming over the hills around them and realized there was no hope of re-supply or rescue. They were prepared to fight to the bitter end, or as he said, "until Hell froze over; then fix bayonets and fight on the ice". They were so cold and tired when word came to withdraw to Hagaru-ri, Ed and most of the Marines didn't want to go. The thought of retreat was abhorrent to everyone with him. Ed felt he would just as soon die on that frozen hill as somewhere down the road.

The only path out of the trap was a narrow 80 mile long road ringed by mountains that were held by the Chinese. More than 7,000 Marines went down that road taking their dead, wounded and all their equipment with them. Against odds of twenty or more to one, they fought every step of the way for the 80 miles to Hangnam and evacuation by sea. When a reporter asked one young Marine what he wanted for Christmas, he replied, "Give me tomorrow."

Ed had been wounded in the shoulder and suffered from frostbite (as nearly all the Marines did). He was shipped to a hospital in Japan and Chosin was his last combat. As a bit of irony, Ed was shipped to the 89th General Hospital in Osaka where

my Mom was working, admitting the wounded. So, Ed, a battle hardened Marine, and I, just a kid, were in Japan at the same
time. It was about seven years before we would meet in that
slop chute at Camp Pendleton.

I don't know what happened to Ed. Just before Christmas he
was transferred to Force Recon at Camp Lejeune, North Carolina
and I never saw him again. More than likely, after all these years,
Ed has answered the final role call. I think about him occasionally and would like to believe he met someone to share his final
years. It would be little enough reward for a hero.

THE CRASH AT CRUSH, TEXAS

The things human beings will do to entertain themselves never ceases to amaze me. A prime example is the publicity stunt that took place on September 15, 1896 in Crush, Texas, one of the state's largest cities.

What? You've never heard of Crush, Texas!? Perhaps that's because Crush, Texas only existed for a single day. The publicity stunt and the city of Crush were the brain child of William George Crush who was a passenger agent for the Missouri-Kansas-Texas Railroad Company—more commonly known as the Katy.

Good thing this isn't a novel. If a fiction writer told a story about a man named Crush who arranged a crash in a city named Crush, no one would believe it. But I assure you this all did happen.

While the Katy brought in over $4 million in passenger sales and freight earnings in 1895, it still had reason to be worried about its future. The economic depression of 1893 saw 25 per cent of the country's railroad companies file for bankruptcy. In Crush's vision, he was certain his proposed stunt would promote the Katy, raise the visibility of his company and assure a stable future.

William Crush realized entertainment for the 2 million settlers in 1890s Texas, was hard to come by. Although railroad accidents were common and deadly in that period, few people had actually seen a train wreck. Purely for the public spectacle, he planned to have two 35-ton locomotives ram headlong into each other.

If nothing else, I suspect Crush was a really good salesman. He managed to sway the Katy owners, convincing them his publicity stunt would reap all sorts of benefits for the railroad.

Crush found two 35-ton steam engines that were being retired for new 60-ton engines and commissioned them for the spectacle. He consulted with company engineers about the safety of the undertaking (only one suggested the collision might cause an explosion, and he was overruled).

A spot about 15 miles north of Waco, Texas was selected for the event. A line of track was laid while the two steam engines were readied for the publicity stunt. Engine No. 1001 was painted red with green trim, while its opponent, No. 999, was painted green with red trim.

Crush immediately got busy preparing the town, which was, of course, named Crush, after him. He drilled two wells and ran pipes for spigots, hired a man from Dallas to run a dozen lemonade stands, brought in tanks of artesian mineral water, erected a restaurant and even a wooden jail that would be patrolled by 200 hired constables. But the main attraction—apart from the trains themselves—was the row of carnival attractions based on Chicago's highly popular Midway at the 1893 World's Fair. "This feature alone will be worth going to Crush City to see," construction foreman A.D. Arbegast told _The Galveston Daily News._

On September 15, the day of the event, spectators poured into the temporary town of Crush, paying $2 to travel there by train from anywhere in Texas. By 10 a.m. a crowd of 10,000 had already arrived, and trains of people kept pulling up every five minutes. "Men, women and children, lawyers, doctors, merchants, farmers, artisans, clerks, representing every class and every grade of society, were scattered around over the hillsides, or clustered around the lunch stands, discussing with eager anticipation the exciting event that they had come so far to see," reported the _Galveston Daily News_.

Unfortunately the collision had to be delayed, because trains were still arriving at the scheduled 4 p.m. show time. Approximately 40,000 people eventually arrived, briefly making Crush the second-largest city in Texas.

At 5:10, Crush himself rode in on a white horse and waved his hat, giving the signal for the engines, pulling an empty boxcar behind each, to start. The engineers and conductors got the behemoths moving, then jumped to safety about 30 yards from the starting point. As the two engines approached, they reached speeds of 50 mph. Their collision was every bit as spectacular as predicted.

A reporter at the scene wrote, "A crash, sound of timbers rent and torn, and then a shower of splinters. There was just a swift instant of silence, and then, as if controlled by a single impulse, both boilers exploded simultaneously and the air was filled with flying missiles of iron and steel varying in size from a postage stamp to half a driving wheel, falling indiscriminately on the just and unjust, the rich and the poor, the great and the small."

At least two people died, and many more were injured by the flying debris and scalding water that erupted from the boilers. J.C. Deane, the Waco photographer hired to take official photos of the crash, lost an eye to a steel bolt. Despite the injuries and shock of violence, the crowd still rushed forward to claim souvenirs from the crash.

William Crush was promptly fired, only to be rehired when managers at the Katy realized how successful the stunt had been in terms of publicity. Despite the accident, the line had become an overnight sensation, catching headlines in the international press. The Missouri-Kansas-Texas went on to expand across the state in the following decades. The Katy not only opened a huge territory, but contributed to the general well-being of its service area by supplying reliable freight and passenger service,

Although the "Crash at Crush" was successful in generating publicity and proved profitable to the railroad, I'm pretty sure no one has attempted that particular publicity stunt again.

THE GREATEST
MARITIME DISASTER

The world's worst maritime disaster happened at the end of World War II, yet the world took little notice of the tragedy. Chances are you've never even heard about the sinking of the *Wilhelm Gustloff*. This is her story.

When Hitler's forces invaded Russian on June 22, 1941 the Russian civilians suffered many acts of cruelty. There certainly was no love lost between the Germans and Russians. When the tide of war changed and the Soviet Union advanced on Germany's eastern front in January of 1945, it was clear the fall of the Third Reich was inevitable. Among the German populace, stories of rape and murder by vengeful Soviet forces inspired dread, which caused many living in the Red Army's path to abandon their homes and make a bid for safety.

The Soviet advance to the south had cut off land routes, so their best chance of escape was on the Baltic Sea and westward toward the relative safety of the German city of Kiel. German civilians seeking an escape from the advancing Soviets converged on the port city of Gotenhafen (now Gdynia, Poland), where the former luxury ocean liner *Wilhelm Gustloff* was docked.

Initially German officials issued and checked for tickets, but in the chaos and panic, the cold, exhausted, hungry and increasingly desperate pressed on board the ship and crammed into any available space. Without a reliable passenger manifest, the exact number of people onboard will never be known. Beyond a doubt when the *Gustloff* sailed at midday on January 30th, it was many times over its intended capacity. Some of the *Gustloff*'s officers estimated the ship—built for less than 2,000 passengers—was carrying at least 10,000 passengers

Early on, the ship's senior officers faced a series of undesirable trade-offs. They could travel through the mine-infested shallower waters, or the submarine-infested deeper waters. Snow, sleet and wind conspired to limit visibility and force the ship into the deeper waters even though adequate escort ships were simply not available. After dark the ship's navigation lights were turned on—increasing visibility, but making the massive ship a beacon for lurking enemy submarines.

Soon the nearby Soviet submarine S-13, under the command of Alexander Marinesko, spotted the large, illuminated ship. It presented an easy target for a commander who could use a boost to his reputation. "He thought he would be a real hero for sinking it."

Shortly after 9 p.m., the S-13 unleashed three torpedoes, each inscribed with messages conveying the Soviets' desire for revenge for the suffering inflicted on the Soviet populace by Nazi forces earlier in the war. Those explosions impacted crew living quarters, the swimming pool area, and the engine room and lower decks, dealing the ship its fatal blows and trapping many occupants with no means of escape.

The *Gustloff* was soon the scene of a mad scramble for survival. Even for those who could get off the mortally wounded ship and seek safety in the open water, the sheer number of passengers far exceeded the capacity of the life rafts. People—many of them children—were trampled to death in an effort to get up the stairs and on to an available lifeboat (the ship was tilted toward the port side, so none of the lifeboats on the starboard side were accessible). The lucky few who managed to get on a boat moving away from the *Gustloff* were assaulted by people who had jumped into the water and now were trying to climb aboard any lifeboat they could reach. Those already in the safety of the lifeboats used oars to beat off those in the water, who were destined to perish.

For those who remained on deck, it was becoming apparent that death in the freezing water was imminent. One of the survivors recounted watching the agonizing decision of a father hanging off the listing ship—still wearing his swastika arm band —to shoot his wife and children. He ran out of bullets before he put the gun to his own head. And then he let go and slid after his dead wife and his children across the icy, snow-covered deck, and over the side.

Just over an hour after the S-13's torpedoes hit, the *Gustloff* slipped beneath the surface.

By the next morning, the waters surrounding the spot where the *Gustloff* went down were filled with bodies, many of them children whose lifejackets caused them to float upside down. Only one known survivor emerged from the floating graveyard —an infant wrapped tightly in blankets aboard a lifeboat, surrounded by deceased passengers. (The officer who found the infant would adopt and raise the boy). Of the passengers who had boarded the previous day a mere fraction—roughly 1,000—had survived.

The sinking of the *Gustloff* is likely the greatest maritime disaster in history. The death toll numbered in the thousands— some put it as high as 9,000—far eclipsing the loss of life from the Titanic and Lusitania combined.

The *Gustloff* was another tragedy in a war full of losses. Even if the details of the *Gustloff's* sinking had been more widely or immediately known, it may not have elicited much sympathy. After years of total war, the public sentiment in the United States and other Allied countries toward the crimes of the Third Reich, suggested even German civilians deserved harsh treatment.

Perhaps now, 75 years later, we might pause a moment to say a prayer for the souls lost that bitter day.

THE EMANCIPATION PROCLAMATION

The history of the Civil War and slavery will probably always be filled with half truths. For example, Abraham Lincoln did not free the slaves (or at least all the slaves) with the Emancipation Proclamation, which he signed on January 1, 1863. The proclamation declared "that all persons held as slaves" _within the rebellious states_ "are, and henceforward shall be free." All slaves were actually made free by the 13th Amendment to the Constitution, which was ratified, after the War, almost 3 years later on December 6, 1865.

Although Lincoln would have liked to free all slaves, he knew it was not possible as long as the Confederacy existed. The real reason for the Emancipation Proclamation was buried deep in the archives of obscure history. Lincoln was a much more astute commander-in-chief then many historians give him credit. He realized enslaved workers constituted not only the backbone of the Confederate war effort, but also the backbone of Robert E. Lee's army.

Although stories of camp slaves with the Confederate armies have faded from our popular memory of the war, anywhere between 6,000 and 10,000 slaves supported Lee's army in various capacities. Many labored as cooks, butchers, blacksmiths, hospital attendants, manual laborers, and thousands of enslaved men accompanied Confederate officers as their camp slaves, or body servants. The North had a large population advantage over the South. Slaves doing most of the Southern army's menial labor freed more soldiers for the actual fighting. For Confederates from Robert E. Lee on down, camp slaves and other enslaved workers—the entire institution of slavery, really—were crucial to the ultimate success of the army in the field and the Confederate insurgency as a whole.

If you remember the history of the period, you know Lee's Army was pretty much making the Union Army look foolish. Lincoln hoped the Proclamation would entice the slaves supporting Lee's Army to desert. The Proclamation, in effect, turned Union armies into armies of liberation, through which newly freed men could look for work in the cities and towns of the North, or even enlist in one of the black regiments forming in the Union army.

News of the Proclamation quickly filtered through Confederate ranks and was certainly discussed among the army's enslaved servants. Lee's decision to bring his army north into free states in early May, following his victory at Chancellorsville, was fraught with danger. His support staff of enslaved labor was at risk of emancipation. However slave owners remained convinced their slaves would remain fiercely loyal even in the face of opportunities to escape. This conviction would be tested throughout the Gettysburg campaign.

When Lee's three corps of infantry, numbering roughly 70,000, crossed the Mason-Dixon Line into Pennsylvania, they encountered clear signs they were no longer in friendly territory. South Carolinians in Lieutenant General James Longstreet's First Corps witnessed the women of Chambersburg, Pennsylvania, appealing to their enslaved servants to run off and seize their freedom.

In the immediate aftermath of the battle and continuing throughout the Confederate army's retreat to Virginia, many slaves abandoned their posts. A quartermaster in John Bell Hood's division observed that "a great many Negroes have gone to the Yankees." This loss of slave labor hampered the retreat of tired Confederates and resulted in additional prisoners being taken, including the camp servants attached to the Richmond Howitzers. Some of these blacks were briefly held as prisoners in Union prison camps. Once released, they joined Union regiments or made their way to towns and cities across the North where they found work.

However, the diaries of many of the Confederate officers indicated their personal slaves remained loyal to their masters. These men chose not to escape, and while there can be little doubt these stories convey evidence of strong bonds between owner and slave, the narrow belief in unwavering loyalty fails to consider other factors that may have influenced their behavior. Some likely anticipated the brutal punishment which would accompany their recapture (or punishment that might be meted out to family members in their absence), while others worried about how they might actually be treated once behind Union lines. I'm sure many had no reason to expect kind treatment at the hands of any white person.

As the Confederate army reorganized in the weeks following the campaign, the thin ranks of many regiments were magnified by the absence of its enslaved. Gettysburg may not have been the great turning point of the war for Lee and the Army of Northern Virginia—after all the army would go on to fight for nearly two more years—but the Gettysburg campaign did signal a crisis of confidence in soldiers' belief in their slaves' unwavering fidelity.

After Gettysburg the Confederate Army was no longer able to fight an offensive war. For the most part they fought defensive actions. I believe this was because Lincoln's Emancipation Proclamation no longer allowed the southerners to trust their supporting slaves.

BANNING SLICED
BREAD

In 1927 Otto F. Rohwedder successfully designed a machine that not only sliced bread loaves, but wrapped them. The first loaf of sliced bread was sold commercially on July 7, 1928 and the bread market would never be the same. Bakeries across the country purchased bread slicing machines and began advertising the pre-cut loaves as "the greatest forward step in the baking industry since bread was wrapped," prompting Americans to coin that immortal phrase: "The greatest thing since sliced bread."

By 1933, even though sliced bread cost more than un-sliced bread (10 cents for a one pound loaf as opposed to 9 cents for an un-sliced loaf) sliced bread sales had exceeded sales of un-sliced loaves. America, particularly the American home maker, was absolutely in love with this innovation.

It would be difficult to find a more patriotic country than the U.S. during World War II. The citizens accepted rationing of commodities such as rubber, gasoline, sugar, butter, eggs, etc. with a bit of grumbling, but tolerated it because the inconvenience was part of their contribution to the war effort. They grew victory gardens and canned the resulting crops so more of the commercially grown produce would be available to feed our fighting troops. Huge numbers invested regularly in war bonds. There was almost no sacrifice the American people wouldn't make for their fighting men and women.

JAMES R. OLSON

I say almost no sacrifice, because in 1943 the government went one step too far. On January 18, 1943, Claude R. Wickard, the U.S. food administrator, got the bright idea to ban pre-sliced bread in America.

Obviously the ban happy bureaucrats had not given any real thought or analysis to the ban on sliced bread. The outcry over the lack of sliced bread, a product Americans no longer wanted to live without, was heard loud and clear in the halls of government. Naturally the first reaction by the bureaucrats was to make excuses and try to justify their decision. They immediately claimed the ban was about the conservation of resources —wax paper, wheat, and steel.

The American public wasn't about to just take the government's word. Sliced bread was simply too important. They demanded proof the sacrifice of their treasured sliced bread was justified in the name of patriotism.

With regards to wax paper conservation, by FDA regulations, pre-sliced bread used much thicker wax paper than loaves sold whole, due to the fact that sliced bread, not surprisingly, goes stale significantly faster than loaves left un-sliced. While this was the official stated reason for the ban, there was actually no shortage of wax paper at the time the ban was put in place. According to the War Production Board, most bread making companies had wax paper supplies on hand to last several months, even if they didn't buy any more during that span.

It has also been suggested that a secondary goal was to try to conserve wheat and to lower bread and flour prices. Around the start of WWII, the Office of Price Administration had authorized an increase in flour prices by about 10%. This naturally resulted in the price of bread increasing. However, when pre-sliced bread was first introduced nation-wide, bread sales drastically increased. So, the bureaucrats figured by banning pre-sliced bread, the amount of bread consumed would go down. This would then reduce the demand for flour and wheat, and, thus, decrease prices for those products while simultaneously increasing stockpiles of wheat.

As with the wax paper reasoning, the idea of conserving wheat seems an odd thing given that, at the time of the ban, the U.S. had stockpiled over 1 billion bushels of wheat. This was enough to meet the United States' needs for about two years, even if no new wheat was harvested over that span.

There may have been something to the ban conserving steel. A regular kitchen knife does a really lousy job of cutting fresh bread, so families all over the country scrambled to obtain bread cutting knives. The demand for bread knives might actually have stressed a small segment of the steel industry, but it's unlikely the war effort would suffer. Although it was true a fair amount of steel was used in constructing each bread slicing machine, it wasn't likely very many, if any, bread slicing machines would need to be produced during the war. Consequently the ban on sliced bread would probably actually cause a slight increase in the consumption of steel.

Governments seldom admit to making a mistake and did not do so this time. However the public was up in arms and the politicians couldn't afford to have the public begin defying their wartime rules. How would the politicians look if the public began questioning, for example, the need for rationing red meat? On March 8, 1943, not quite three months after the ban on sliced bread was put into place, it was rescinded. Upon lifting the ban, Wickard stated, "Our experience with the order, however, leads us to believe that the savings are not as much as we expected..."

I suspect that's as close to an apology as we'll ever get from any government. However it's unlikely the government will try to ban sliced bread again.

THE LIMPING LADY

If you've never heard of Virginia Hall that'll probably change in the near future. I understand a book and a movie will be available soon and the whole world will have an opportunity to learn about this remarkable woman. She's the only civilian woman to ever be awarded the Distinguished Service Cross (the Army's second highest award) for valor, she was recognized as an honorary Member of the Order of the British Empire, and the Nazi German regime considered her the most dangerous Allied spy.

Virginia was born April 6, 1906 in Baltimore, Maryland. In college she studied foreign languages including French, German, and Italian. With her parents' support, Hall went to Europe and traveled extensively on the Continent, studying in Austria, France, and Germany in the late 1920s, with the goal of working in the diplomatic corps. Unfortunately her diplomatic career was over before it began.

In 1932, Virginia was the victim of a hunting accident resulting in the amputation of her left leg just below the knee. She obtained a prosthesis, but artificial limbs in the 1930s were not much further advanced than the traditional pirate's peg leg. The wooden leg, which she nicknamed "Cuthbert", allowed her to walk, but was not very comfortable. It was attached with leather straps and when climbing up or down steps, the leather would chafe the skin until it was raw and the stump would blister and bleed. It would have been extremely difficult going down steps because the leg's ankle didn't work the way our ankles do, and she always felt vulnerable to falling forward.

In 1940, as the war spread through Europe, Virginia volunteered for the Special Operations Executive (SOE)—the British espionage organization. Virginia Hall admittedly made an unlikely spy. British Prime Minister Winston Churchill's war cabinet had forbidden women from serving on the frontlines, and some within the SOE questioned whether Virginia was fit to be operating in the midst of a resistance operation. It wasn't only her gender, but her wooden leg caused her to walk with a limp, making her dangerously conspicuous. Although the SOE wasn't certain a woman could be a successful spy, they needed someone who spoke fluent French, and Virginia spoke like a native.

In early September 1941, Virginia arrived in Vichy France on a clandestine and perilous mission. She had been tasked with organizing local resistance networks against France's German occupiers and communicating intelligence to the SOE. In reality, however, Virginia Hall's supervisors were not particularly hopeful about her prospects; they didn't expect her to survive more than a few days in a region teeming with Gestapo agents. Indeed, Virginia quickly became known as the "Limping Lady" of Lyon, the French city where she set up base.

Virginia managed to survive more than a few days. In fact she spent over a year in Vichy France, working to coordinate the activities of the French Resistance. She worked primarily in and around Toulouse and Lyon, involving the delivery of money and agents to the French spy networks.

When she was forced to flee in 1942 it was because Klaus Barbie (who would become known as the Butcher of Lyon), became the Nazi Gestapo chief of German-occupied Lyon. He immediately put out posters with Virginia's picture and made an all out effort to capture the dangerous spy. She narrowly escaped Lyon by train, then disappeared into the Pyrenees Mountains in an attempt to reach neutral Spain.

Crossing the Pyrenees on foot would have been difficult for an able bodied soldier. It must have been nearly impossible for Virginia. The grinding, relentless climb and then the grinding, relentless descent would have been agonizing with her artificial leg. After the war she told her niece crossing the mountains was the worst part of the war.

She was briefly arrested for crossing into Spain illegally, but was released with the help of the American embassy. For about a year, she worked with the SOE based out of Madrid, then returned to London, where she was recognized as an honorary Member of the Order of the British Empire.

After completing her work with the SOE, Virginia's spy career wasn't over. She joined the equivalent American organization, the Office of Strategic Services, Special Operations Branch (the forerunner of the Central Intelligence Agency—CIA), and requested a chance to return to France, which was still under Nazi occupation. Granting her request, the OSS sent her to Brittany, France, with a false identity and a code name.

Over the course of the next year, Virginia mapped out safe zones for supply drops and safe houses. She worked with Operation Jedburgh, which was a clandestine operation in which personnel were dropped by parachute into occupied France, the Netherlands and Belgium to conduct sabotage and guerrilla warfare, and to lead the local resistance forces in actions against the Germans. Virginia personally helped train Resistance fighters in guerilla warfare, and sent a constant stream of reports back to Allied intelligence. Her work continued up until the very end of the war. She only ceased once Allied forces caught up to her and her team in September 1945.

Upon returning to the United States, Virginia married Paul Goillot, a former OSS operative himself. The pair both transitioned into work at the Central Intelligence Agency, where Virginia and her husband were assigned to the Special Activities Division, focused on covert operations. After fifteen years at the CIA, she retired in 1966, moving with her husband to a Barnesville, Maryland farm. She died July 8, 1982 (aged 76) in Rockville, Maryland, and is buried nearby.

Many of Virginia's exploits have never been told, and some are still classified. Virginia's refusal to talk and write about her

World War II experiences resulted in her slipping into obscurity during her lifetime. The world at large may have forgotten Virginia, but the CIA did not. In 2016, a CIA field agent training facility was named the Virginia Hall Expeditionary Center. The CIA Museum has only awarded five operatives individual sections in its catalog. Four are men who went on to head the CIA. The fifth is the Limping Lady, Virginia Hall. She was also inducted into the Maryland Women's Hall of Fame in 2019.

Many war heroes have become disabled because of their service. I believe the Limping Lady may actually be the only one who went to war after she was disabled.

TOYS FOR TOTS

History isn't only about celebrities and disasters; it's about people just like you and me. The best history stories are when ordinary people take the time and make the effort to help people they don't even know. That's exactly what my favorite charity, Toys for Tots, is all about. If I could make the world a place where every child has a wonderful, carefree childhood, I would do so in a heartbeat. We all know some children never have that idyllic life. Yet Toys For Tots gives many children the gift of experiencing Christmas and having childhood memories to look back on.

In 1947 Diane Hendricks had created a few handcrafted dolls and asked her husband, Marine Corps Reserve Major Bill Hendricks to deliver them to an agency that supports children in need. When Bill reported back that he couldn't find such an organization, she instructed him to "start one!" Even a Marine isn't brave enough to say "no" to his wife. Major Hendricks immediately enlisted help from the men in his Los Angeles reserve unit to establish the basis of what would become Toys For Tots. For Christmas 1947 the Marines collected and distributed 5,000 toys to children in need.

In 1948 Commandant of the Marine Corps, Lieutenant General Vandegrift, took note of the successful community engagement and directed all Marine Reserve Units to implement a Toys For Tots campaign, transforming it into a national community action program.

Bill Hendrick's civilian job was Director of Public Relations at

Warner Brothers Studios. He was friends with many celebrities he asked to help support the newly created Marine Toys for Tots Program. As a favor to Bill, Walt Disney designed the first Toys for Tots poster, which included a miniature three-car train that was subsequently adopted as the Toys for Tots logo.

Beginning with the distribution of 5,000 toys to needy children in 1947 the Marine Toys for Tots Program currently distributes an average of 18 million toys to 7 million less fortunate children annually.

This is not a story about a charity. It's a story about Christmas and the wonderful things Christmas brings to each of us. Did your Mother tell you it's more blessed to give than to receive? Well, she was right, as these four stories from the Toys For Tots website attest. I realize some public relations guy could have written all of these stories, but I believe they're true. After all, if you can't believe a Marine, who can you believe?

Story Contributed By – Ms. Janel Doyle, Bowling Green, KY.
Each year, our local Toys for Tots partners with the local Law Enforcement and Fire Departments to ensure less fortunate children in our community have a Merry Christmas. This past year, employees from our Regional Jail decided to give families food for Christmas, so they drove around the lower income part of town and delivered baskets full of food to various families. After they delivered food to a family of five, they contacted me asking if Toys for Tots would be able to provide the family with toys since they did not see any gifts for Christmas in their home. After obtaining the address from the jail employee, I went to the home and was met by a beautiful mother holding a baby. I told her who I was and that I wanted to give the children toys on behalf of Toys for Tots if that was okay. She stood there for a minute speechless with a smile on her face as a tear rolled down her cheek, and said "yes, please". I got the ages and gender of the children and went to our warehouse to bag the toys and grabbed a couple of bikes for the two older children. I returned with a member from the Marine Corps League, and as we entered her

home, my eyes were fixed on the Christmas tree that was made of a cut-out sheet that was duct taped to her living room wall. A single string of lights was plugged in and made an outline on the "sheet" tree. Under the tree were three small packages: one for each child, and there was nothing but a couch and a TV in the living room. As we brought in the gifts and bikes, the children were wrapped around their mother's legs in amazement. Their eyes sparkled, smiles were contagious, and the mother had more tears. This is why we work tirelessly for those needing Christmas help, and pouring our hearts and souls into Toys for Tots.

Story Contributed By – Sunny Helstrom, Fort Wayne, IN. I was contacted by a mother who was going to college and suddenly found herself in need of assistance. After speaking with her I learned she had recently gone through brain surgery to remove a brain tumor which left her with short term memory loss and seizures. Because of this, she was no longer able to continue her dream of becoming a nurse or even perform everyday tasks. She was unable to provide presents for her five year old daughter. The day she came to pick up her toys for her little girl was one of the most heartwarming days of the campaign. Once we gave her the toys, I asked her if by chance her little girl would like a bicycle. She became so emotional and explained her daughter had recently begged for a bike, but she could not afford one. The mother wept and thanked us repeatedly! She humbly asked if she could give me and Joyce a hug, and then said, "I wish there was a way I could thank all those involved". I told her not to worry, that I would make sure they all knew how grateful and appreciative she was!

Teri Roundtree, Wolfe City, TX . A child and the story that stands out is of an autistic girl in our county, she is non-verbal and 13 years old. Her mother said she still believes in Santa. We made arrangement for our Santa, Mr. Bill Gaston, to deliver toys to this girl's house. It was extremely uplifting to see the shine and surprise in the little girl's face and eyes. As it came time for us to leave, the young lady looked at Santa and said, "Thank You", and gave him a hug. We all choked back tears. Our crew, Santa, Mom... all of us. Our little non-verbal, autistic girl managed to find the courage to speak to Santa, it was amazing.

Teri Roundtree, Wolfe City, TX . A young man and his wife that were walking down the sidewalk outside of our warehouse really stand out in my mind. I was trying to communicate over the phone with a Spanish speaking family to have them come pick up toys. At the time, no one at the warehouse spoke Spanish. I asked the young couple walking down the sidewalk if either spoke Spanish, and the young lady did. She took over the phone call and informed the family their toys were ready. I said thanks and thought they would be on their way, but it turned out they were at the warehouse to pick up toys as well. So, we gave them their toys and wished them a good night.

About an hour later, the young man came back to our warehouse. He came in with his head down, kind of trembling. He looked up with tears in his eyes and said, "My wife and I were being children when we got home. We opened the bags to see what our kids were getting for Christmas, and I had to come back and say thank you. Our kids have never, ever had a Christmas like this." That couple walked close to 30 minutes one way on a cold night to get those toys. He then walked back to the warehouse to thank us.

When we started this journey, our entire team knew it was a good thing. We knew we were helping children. We had no idea how much we were helping parents.

****

I hope these stories reminded each of us what the Christmas season is about. Because of the COVID-19 virus, Toys for Tots has had to adjust the way they do business to keep everyone safe and healthy. However, I assure you they will still make certain every child will be able to open a present. In the same spirit, will you please make a special effort to share something with someone—even if it's just a smile or a kind word.

Have a blessed and joyous Christmas. As Tiny Tim said, "God Bless us, everyone!"

THE YOUNGEST HERO

Nobody knows how many underage boys lied about their ages and joined military service during World War II. America was still in the throes of the Great Depression when the war began, and some of those boys had come from large families where there wasn't enough food to go around. Others just wanted to get away from family problems. In 1991 Ray Jackson, who had joined the Marines at 16 during World War II, founded the group, Veterans of Underage Military Service, and claimed more than 1,200 active members (that's almost certainly not all the underage warriors who served in WWII).

I'm pretty sure Calvin Graham, born April 3, 1930 in Canton, Texas, was not a member of Ray Jackson's group, but he did lie about his age when he enlisted. Calvin was probably the youngest boy (it would be hard to imagine anyone younger) to serve during WW II, but we know for certain he was the youngest to be decorated for bravery and awarded the Purple Heart for wounds received in action.

Calvin Graham, one of seven children, was just 11 years old in the sixth grade in Crocket, Texas, when he hatched his plan to lie about his age and join the Navy. At 5-foot-2 and just 125 pounds, Graham dressed in an older brother's clothes and fedora and went to the Navy Recruiting Office in Houston. Graham recounted years later, he stood in line with a number of young boys he knew for certain were only 14 to 15. He maintained the Navy knew he and the others in line that day were underage, "but we were losing the war then, so they took six of us." Calvin told his mother he was going to visit relatives. Instead, he dropped out of the seventh grade and shipped off to San Diego for basic training. There, he said, the drill instructors were aware of the underage recruits and often made them run extra miles and lug heavier packs.

The newly christened battleship *USS South Dakota* steamed out of Philadelphia in August of 1942. Aboard was a gunner from Texas who would soon become the nation's youngest decorated war hero. Calvin Graham, the fresh-faced seaman, was only 12 years old.

The *South Dakota* joined the bitter Guadalcanal campaign in November, 1942. During one of the naval engagements, a Japanese ship locked its searchlights on the *South Dakota*, and the ship took 42 enemy hits. Graham was manning his gun when shrapnel tore through his jaw and mouth. Another hit knocked him down, and he fell through three stories of superstructure. Dazed and bleeding the 12 year-old made it to his feet and helped pull other crew members to safety. He took belts off the dead and made tourniquets for the living. He gave the wounded cigarettes and encouragement all night in spite of his own wounds. Shrapnel had knocked out Calvin's front teeth, and he had flash burns from the hot guns. A corpsman "fixed me up with salve and a coupla stitches," he recalled. "I didn't do any complaining because half the ship was dead."

The South Dakota limped back to dry-dock for repairs while the wounded crew members went to the hospital for treatment. While Calvin was recuperating, he was awarded a Bronze Star with a "V" for valor, as well as a Purple Heart for his injuries. What should have been a joyous occasion was about to become a nightmare.

Calvin's mother, who didn't know her son had gone to war, recognized her boy in newsreel footage. She contacted the naval authorities, revealing Calvin's true age. The wounded hero was immediately arrested, returned to Texas and thrown in a brig at Corpus Christi, Texas, where he languished for almost three months.

Calvin managed to get a message to his sister Pearl, who complained to the newspapers that the Navy was mistreating a decorated sailor simply because he had enlisted while underage. In order to avoid a publicity firestorm, the Navy voided Calvin's enlistment, stripping him of his medals and benefits before simply tossing him from jail with a suit and a few dollars in his pocket. He was released two days before his thirteenth birthday, the youngest veteran of the war, with few prospects ahead of him. The only work he could find was selling magazine subscriptions.

What happens to soldiers once the wars end, the parades pass by and the accolades fade away? The rent is still due, the old injuries still ache and the nightmares remain. In Calvin Graham's case he spent the remainder of his life trying to reclaim the honors he had earned.

In 1948, Graham joined the Marines—legally. He served honorably until 1951 when his back was seriously injured in an accident while on duty. He was medically discharged from the Marines, but the problems surrounding his prior discharge from the Navy prevented him from receiving veterans' medical benefits. He eventually gained only limited disability benefits.

Over the years Calvin Graham continued to fight for justice from the government that had betrayed his sacrifice. A few people in high places took up his cause and in 1978, President Jimmy Carter signed a bill returning all of Graham's medals except the Purple Heart. Ten years later, President Ronald Reagan signed legislation approving disability benefits, back pay and reimbursements for medical costs stemming from his injuries. Even then, he only received a fraction of what he was owed.

In 1988 Hollywood made Calvin Graham's story into a popular made-for-TV movie, "Too Young the Hero". The fates remained against Calvin. Writers and agents took huge shares of the money he received for the rights to his story, and in the end, he only received $15,000.

Calvin Graham died on November 6, 1992 from heart failure. If there were such a diagnosis as a broken heart, that should have been Calvin's cause of death. At the age of 12, Calvin Graham broke the law to serve his country, during a time when the U.S. military might well be accused of having had a "don't ask, don't tell" policy with regard to underage enlistees. He served with honor and distinction, before his country turned its back on him. It wasn't until 1994, two years after he died, that the military relented and returned the seaman's last medal —his Purple Heart.

Although Calvin Graham had every right to be bitter about how the military had treated him, he never regretted having shed blood for his beloved country.

A CHRISTMAS
MIRACLE

In the summer of 1914, after the assassination of the Arch-duke Ferdinand, the countries of Europe enthusiastically went to war. No one realized how bloody the prolonged conflict would become, but they were beginning to learn. Within only a few months thousands of soldiers had been killed in heavy fighting, resulting in a bloody stalemate, with a front that stretched from the Swiss border to the North Sea.

By December 1914 the reality of trench warfare had settled in. Weeks of heavy rain had turned both the trenches and the No Man's Land that separated them into a cold, muddy morass. For those in the trenches, daily life was a miserable existence of cold and mud, hunger and trench foot. Over everything was the stink of decaying corpses and untreated sewage. However, it was a misery shared by enemies who were, in some places, separated by less than 50 yards. The men in the trenches had seen battle, but they had not yet lost their humanity to the horrors World War I would produce.

On December 7th Pope Benedict XV, who had ascended to the papacy just a month after the outbreak of war, issued an appeal to the leaders of Europe "that the guns may fall silent, at least upon the night the angels sang". Benedict's hope was that a truce would allow the warring powers to negotiate a fair and lasting peace. However no leaders from either side showed any interest in the Pope's appeal. After all, no one was going to be shooting

JAMES R. OLSON

at them and they wouldn't personally do any fighting.

It's likely the Generals and politicians realized if their troops stopped killing each other and were allowed to fraternize, the troops would soon realize the men they fought so viciously were human beings with hopes, dreams, and families waiting for them back home. Obviously it would be more difficult to aggressively attack a foe you sympathized with.

As December 25th approached, the constant soaking rain gave way to frost, and the battlefields of Flanders were blanketed with a light dusting of snow. Then, as sometimes happens, outside events transpired which provided a path to the truce their leaders had rejected.

German Kaiser Wilhelm II sent Christmas trees to the front in an effort to bolster morale. On December 23rd German soldiers began placing the trees, decorated with whatever ornaments the soldiers could devise, outside their trenches. They sang hymns such as "Stille Nacht", and voices from the Allied lines responded with Christmas carols of their own. While there were relatively few British troops who spoke German, many Germans had worked in Britain before the war, and this experience facilitated communication between the two groups. An impromptu truce began with such simple things as shared Christmas carols and open conversation.

By Christmas Eve, some lower-ranking British officers had begun ordering their men not to fire unless fired upon. Even though the officers' decisions were made without any authorization from above, a tenuous truce slowly began to take hold. A true Christmas miracle was about to happen.

As morning broke on Christmas Day, German soldiers emerged from their trenches, waving their arms to demonstrate they had no ill intent. When it became clear they were not carrying weapons, British soldiers soon joined them, meeting in No Man's Land to socialize and exchange gifts. Small groups even gathered to sing carols, half singing in English and half in German. Even with the mixed languages, it sounded beautiful. Each side agreed no hostilities would resume without giving a

166

fair warning.

British soldiers wrote home of sharing food and drink with men who had been, just a day earlier, their mortal enemies. The men themselves could scarcely believe the remarkable events that were transpiring around them and they recognized, even while it was happening, their unique and historic significance. The 1st Battalion of The Royal Welch Fusiliers played a football match with the German Battalion 371. The Germans won 2–1. However, all was not frivolity. One of the most common activities in areas observing the Christmas Truce was joint services to bury the dead.

It would be too much to expect the war to halt everywhere. The pause in fighting was not universally observed, nor had it been sanctioned anywhere by commanders on either side. Along some two-thirds of the 30-mile front controlled by the British Expeditionary Force, the guns fell silent. The truce was not widely adopted in French-controlled areas. German soldiers had spent the summer overrunning a huge swath of French territory, and the animosity toward the occupiers was too strong. There was also no truce on the Eastern Front, as Russia was still operating under the Julian calendar, and the Russian Orthodox Christmas would not be observed until early January.

In the days following Christmas, violence returned to the Western Front, although the truce persisted until after New Year's Day in some areas. While the truce could not have succeeded without the endorsement of junior officers on both sides, British and German generals quickly took steps to prevent any further episodes of fraternization between their men. Still, there were no courts-martial or punishments linked to the events of the Christmas Truce. Senior commanders likely recognized the disastrous effect such a move would have on morale in the trenches. After this Christmas miracle there were no more truces or breaks in the fighting until the armistice on November 11, 1918.

Judging by the bloody fighting over the remainder of the war, the opposing armies apparently had no difficulty resuming their jobs of killing each other after the Christmas truce. Wouldn't it have been wonderful if the soldiers in the trenches had decided to lay down their arms permanently and left the politicians to fight the war?

AFTERWORD

If you enjoyed this book, please consider posting a review on Amazon. Even if it's only a few sentences, it would be a huge help for other readers when they make a decision whether a book is worth reading.